ENDORSEMENTS

MW00938097

By comparing the physical *core* of the human body to the spiritual *core* of a believer, co-authors Kelly Dean and Sharon Czerwien encourage Christians to strengthen the crucial areas of their life. Using personal examples, illustrations from biblical characters, and pointing us to God and His word, we are shown how we can build up those critical areas of our spiritual *core* and learn to face the bumps in our lives with hope.

~Dr. Jon Konnerup,
Baptist Bible Fellowship International,
Mission Director

Sharon has written a delightful book. With down to earth, real-life illustrations and helpful analogies, she communicates essential truths in a manner that makes them easy to access and apply in one's own life. She provides a helpful breakdown of 'counseling categories' including seeing a professional biblical counselor when needed. This book is chock full of tips and insights to help keep our perspective centered on God's character, especially his goodness and sovereignty, even in the messiness and hard times that life often brings. This book will be a blessing to those who read it.

~Dr. Bryan Warren, LPC;
Instructor of Counseling,
Western Seminary

Upon reading this book, "Core: Biblical Principles for When Life Gets Bumpy" I was immediately encouraged to enlist others to do this Bible study as a group. I found it enlightening and encouraging to see well-written, Bible-based studies for our Christian women today. I also know what it is to be shaken to the *core* mentally, physically, and spiritually, but because of my husband who never gave up on me, and daily read the Word, he caused me to remember God. You certainly will be blessed reading Sharon's writing from a spiritual view as well as a Christian therapist's outlook on the physical aspect.

~Carol R. Levergood,
50 years in ministry including
Missionary 21 years in Brazil
and author of *Green Bananas*

I am a mother of nine and let me tell you, parenting is filled with circumstances and events that jostle our inner being. Wouldn't it be wonderful to correlate those challenges to some reason for their existence? Sharon does just that as she helps connect the dots between pain and purpose; "bumps", as she calls them, are useful. I found that the chapters' end questions further strengthen my understanding of God's continual hand in my mothering journey. Does your spiritual *core* feel floppy? This book presents the practical connection between knowing the Word and resting in the truth of Scripture.

~Pam Fields,
Host of "The Mom Next Door,
Stories of Faith" Podcast;
Blogger at www.tendingfields.net

CORE

CORE

Biblical Principles for
When Life Gets Bumpy

Sharon Czerwien and Kelly Dean

XULON PRESS

Xulon Press
2301 Lucien Way #415
Maitland, FL 32751
407.339.4217
www.xulonpress.com

© 2021 by Sharon Czerwien and Kelly Dean

All rights reserved solely by the author. The author guarantees all
contents are original and do not infringe upon the legal rights of
any other person or work. No part of this book may be reproduced
in any form without the permission of the author.

Due to the changing nature of the Internet, if there are any web
addresses, links, or URLs included in this manuscript, these may
have been altered and may no longer be accessible. The views
and opinions shared in this book belong solely to the author and
do not necessarily reflect those of the publisher. The publisher
therefore disclaims responsibility for the views or opinions
expressed within the work.

Unless otherwise indicated, Scripture quotations taken from the
New King James Version (NKJV). Copyright © 1982 by Thomas
Nelson, Inc. Used by permission. All rights reserved.

Paperback ISBN-13: 978-1-66282-645-0
Ebook ISBN-13: 978-1-66282-646-7

TABLE OF CONTENTS

Introduction

IMAGINE YOU ARE driving. You are late again and turn down a road with speed bumps. Not something else to slow you down this morning! Does anyone like speed bumps? It is important to consider the *value* or *purpose* of the speed bumps. They are designed to help control one's speed, especially in a neighborhood or school complex. When you associate safety to speed bumps it makes them a bit more bearable.

In life, we experience spiritual *bumps* along the way, too! Trials enter. Times get tough. Life may frustrate or overwhelm you. These trials may feel like *simple*—but annoying—neighborhood speed bumps, or more like a drive through miles and miles of a bumpy construction zone with no end in sight.

Throughout this book, trials will be considered life's *bumps*. These trials may be physical, emotional, spiritual, or a combination. These are the types of things we figuratively *drive through* in life, and we often have no control over them. These bumps may make us uncomfortable, angry, discouraged, anxious, etc. Lord-willing, as we mature spiritually, these bumps will grow our faith instead of drive us off course.

Sometimes, we just need a good reminder that these trials serve a purpose, just like the speed bumps.

God works in mysterious ways. He brought Kelly Dean and me (Sharon Czerwien) together as the result of a car accident (a literal *bump* in my life). Kelly was my physical therapist in Spring of 2020. I was fascinated by the physical *core* and how it impacts so much of one's physical body. In treatment, Kelly worked with me to strengthen my physical *core*, which helped my lower back heal. While I was going through this healing process, I kept thinking: *Wow, the core is incredibly vital to the workings of the entire body! There are so many spiritual applications!*

Since I had just been in a car accident prior to doing physical therapy, the idea of *bumps* was often on my mind. The results from this accident caused specific trials in my life, but I was positively challenged by the overlapping concepts of the physical and spiritual *core*. Later that year, I approached Kelly and invited her to provide details about the physical *core* for this book.

During this same timeframe, I was also blessed to be under the discipleship of Biblical Counselor, Rosalie Francetich. She helped me work through some anxieties that stemmed from my car accident. Some of what I learned from Rosalie will be mentioned in this book.

Since Jesus often used comparisons and analogies in His earthly ministry, Kelly and I thought it ideal to use analogies throughout the book, thus the ideas of *bumps* and *core*. Kelly will walk through the intricacies of the physical *core*. I will then cover the spiritual *core*. With a proper spiritual *core*, the trials that arise will not overwhelm or destroy us spiritually.

Our *core* is our everything! We will learn from Kelly that the physical *core* provides stability, among other important benefits. The same holds true for our spiritual *core*. Since both are of such importance in life (and for this book), *core* will be italicized each time it appears.

The book will have three main sections:

- The Physical *Core*

Kelly will walk through her journey with specific problems arising in her own physical *core*. She will then work through the layers and purposes of the physical *core*.

- The Spiritual *Core*

I will walk through the correlations between the physical and spiritual *core*. I will cover the following *core* spiritual principles that can help us respond properly in our life's *bumps*.

1. God is sovereign.

2. Trials have purpose.

3. Our faith must stay rooted in God.

4. Our heart can cause problems.

5. Perseverance is necessary in our journey.

Principles #1 and #2 will help us to look *upward* as we study what the Bible teaches about God's workings in our life.

Principles #3 and #4 will help us look *inward*. We will consider the *result* of applying the first two principles. We will also discover what is inside each of us that can get us into spiritual trouble.

We will then study principle #5 and learn what the Bible teaches about perseverance.

- The Application

We will consider three categories of spiritual help and conclude with practical strategies to help us either stay on or get back on course.

Kelly and I pray that you find encouragement as we delve into key Biblical principles to hold onto when life gets *bumpy*.

Since Kelly has written chapters 1-2, the use of "I" in these chapters will be Kelly. Since I (Sharon) have written the remaining chapters, the "I" will represent Sharon in the remainder of the book.

Section 1
The Physical *Core*

Personal Struggle

Core WEAKNESS AND low back pain is an epidemic in our culture. So much so, most people do not even acknowledge it as an issue. It is simply understood that *everyone has back pain.* Were our bodies designed to thrive with an *acceptable* level of back pain?

I (Kelly) felt like my body was falling apart and desperately struggled to find a way to fix it. We all have a story, and my story, like many, was filled with speed bumps and unexpected potholes. The bumps in my life (injuries, sexual abuse, infertility, and physical brokenness) became a part of God's plan for my ministry and my work. My journey of learning how to heal my body physically, and help others heal, has been completely directed by God and has included far more than simply knowing the muscles and how they work. Along this journey God has used the unexpected difficulties in my life to help me seek a deep understanding of the foundational *core* strength that all of us seek.

As I look at my story from the beginning, it is easy to see how God had a purpose in all the trials and difficulties. I can see how He used my personality, my experiences, my spiritual gifts, my strengths, and my weaknesses as a tool for His purposes. I had no idea how all these pieces of my life would impact my *core* and would ultimately lead to my ministry, but God did.

How My Childhood and Young Adult Life Impacted My *Core*

My story of my *core* began in my childhood. I did not grow up knowing the Lord. I was a child of a single mom and was exposed to many situations from which a young girl should have been protected. Sadly, I experienced sexual abuse as a child, and I learned to numb myself to unpleasant circumstances. I learned at a young age to be independent, self-sufficient, and careful. I also learned to ignore pain.

In childhood, my body was athletic, yet vulnerable to injury. I consistently sprained wrists and ankles during gymnastics and ice hockey. I did not find my niche in a sport until my stepfather introduced me to competitive swimming. I started later than most but excelled quickly. Swimming was a sport my body could do, without injury. Swimming quickly became my refuge, the pool my *god*, and my accomplishments my identity. I could push myself and accomplish great things and be independent at the same time.

Swimming also provided opportunities. I received a full athletic scholarship to the University of New Mexico. My identity became more deeply entrenched in my athletic abilities, and I continued to push myself to new levels. As part of collegiate swimming training, we did a *crazy-amount* of crunches, dry land kicking, and v-sits. In all, we did a lot of traditional (and not-so-traditional) ab work. I was in incredible shape with a strong *core*. During those years, I believed I was invincible, and my body could do anything I pushed it to do.

I thrived in that environment, until one day during swim team practice, I partially dislocated my shoulder. It was devastating. Even though I was in incredible shape, my joints and ligaments were very loose, and the way I trained myself only reinforced my mentality to ignore pain. By some miracle, I was able to rest and rehabilitate my shoulder effectively and still compete in my last conference championships as a senior; however, this injury greatly impacted my *invincibility* belief. My identity and my *god* started to shift. The identity I found in sports started to shift.

The injuries I endured influenced my career path. My personal rehabilitation experiences led me to pursue a career in Physical Therapy. I do not believe I would have become a physical therapist if I had not experienced the injuries that I had as a child and young adult.

I attended graduate school at University of North Dakota and received my Master of Physical Therapy in the Spring of 1997. I immediately developed a passion for neurology and neuro-muscular reeducation. I trained to work primarily with stroke and brain injury patients (adults, elderly, kids, and even newborns). For the first 7-8 years of my career, this was my specialty and became my new identity. I no longer relied on my body to help me achieve my dreams, I now relied on my brain. I became highly specialized and dove into my career. It was challenging but rewarding work. My identity shifted from being a swimmer to being a physical therapist, but I still did not believe I needed God.

How Motherhood Impacted My *Core* and Led Me to Christ

When I was 27, I experienced my first miscarriage. I had been married for several years. Up until this point, I lived my life believing if

I simply worked hard enough, I could achieve my goals. The concept of losing a baby never occurred to me. The loss dramatically impacted my independent, self-reliant belief system and shook my identity to the *core*. For the first time, I realized that I was not in control of my life.

I experienced additional fertility struggles, and that added strain to my already shaken marriage. My son was finally conceived, but his birth was extremely difficult. I once again realized that I could not just force my life to go in the direction I wanted. Birth is not some swim race that I could just power through and make happen. After a difficult labor experience, my son was born via c-section. I felt like my body failed me. I had a long history of not dealing with pain; so I continued to ignore my feelings and pushed forward. I fell in love with my boy and motherhood and believed that I had faced my speed bump, and life would now continue as I desired. Proverbs 16:9 reads, "A man's heart plans his way, but the LORD directs his steps."

At 28, I experienced another miscarriage, and my marriage shattered. My husband decided he wanted a divorce, and my world imploded. This was the moment that I finally let my guard down and allowed Jesus to enter my heart and take over my life. It was the most difficult season, yet the most meaningful season of my life. I was heartbroken *and* rescued all at the same time. I surrendered to the realization that I am not actually in control of my life, but that God is good and has a plan. The truth that God would never leave me alone to figure it out on my own changed the entire direction of my life. Jeremiah 29:11 reads, "For I know the thoughts that I think toward you, says the LORD..."

Old Patterns Die Hard

Several years later, I married a believer and moved across the country and started a journey to build our family. Even though I had given God control over my life, this did not mean that my journey into motherhood was automatically bump free. Sadly, the journey to growing my family was a roller coaster of fear, hope, blessing, disappointment, joy, heartache, and disconnection. I suffered from several more miscarriages and ended up becoming pregnant eight times in twelve years. Five of those babies are in heaven, and three I have been able to hold and raise. This was one of the most challenging times of my life—emotionally, physically, and spiritually.

Physically, I thought I was in great shape when I got pregnant with my son, but in hindsight, I am certain my *core* issues became apparent after this first full-term pregnancy. Each pregnancy added more fear, emotional pain, and physical disconnect. By the time I was in the 3rd trimester of my second full term pregnancy, I looked like I was having triplets. My tummy was so big, and my *core* was very weak. I was able to have a successful delivery with her, but it was difficult and led to a challenging birth recovery. My physical *core* was destroyed after that birth.

I still did not understand what my body needed. My history of athletic striving and powering through life impacted my ability to use my *core* the way God designed it. The result had lasting effects on my body and ultimately how I lived my life. I tried to rebuild the strength I knew I was missing, but I did all the wrong things. I exercised in unhealthy ways, and everything I knew from fitness and my physical therapy career seemed lost on me.

In addition, I got pregnant again and again and lost two more babies. By the time I was pregnant with my youngest daughter (third full term pregnancy), I was so broken spiritually, emotionally, and physically that I was unable to connect to my body or the baby at all. Fear consumed me, and I became numb. My *core* was numb too. This low point led me to prayer and counseling. By God's grace, I experienced a great amount of healing, emotionally and spiritually, during this pregnancy and was able to have a beautiful birth. However, I still had no real insight on how to reconnect physically with my *core*.

After one more loss, we stepped off the fertility roller coaster and decided to focus on the babies we had and allow my body and heart to heal. At the time, I was so used to powering through pain that I did not realize how motherhood had really taken its toll on my body. Regardless of how much I exercised and tried to fix my body with traditional ab work, I kept getting more disconnected from my *core*. I developed constant low back pain, pelvic instability, abdominal pain, intestinal issues, pelvic floor weakness, and a weak bulging tummy. I felt old, weak, hopeless, and broken. I desperately returned to my old "power-through-life" mentality, and my body was no longer willing to respond.

My Small Glimpse of Hope

Just when I thought this was how my life was going to be, God gave me a glimpse of hope through a *chance* meeting with my sister-in-law (also a physical therapist). While at a family Thanksgiving, I was sharing my issues. She took one look at my tummy and said, "I know what is wrong with your tummy; you have a diastasis." (A diastasis is a separation in the muscles of the abdominal wall that keeps the *core* from holding you together.) A light bulb went on. Yes, I am a

PT. Yes, we learned (very briefly) about diastasis recti in school. And no, I had not even considered that this was what was happening to my *core*. At the time I had no idea how this could be connected to my other issues.

My sister-in-law measured my diastasis and was nothing short of horrified at what she found. She simply said it was the most severe separation she had ever felt. I would need surgery to repair it. I was relieved by this news. I was desperate, falling apart, and felt like I was working hard and going nowhere. It was validating to have something medically wrong with me and to let someone else (a surgeon) be responsible for fixing it.

I got a second opinion from another PT whom I respected. She confirmed the diagnosis and felt it was the worst separation that *she* had ever felt. She instructed me to put on a girdle, stop all exercise, and consult a surgeon. I started to feel less validated and a bit scared.

My primary care doctor gave me the same advice and referred me to a plastic surgeon. The appointment with the plastic surgeon was mortifying. He did not care about my pain, my weakness, my inability to do basic movements without falling apart. He only told me how he could give me a tummy tuck and make it all look better. He was more than happy to do the surgery, and it would cost about $10,000 because this surgery is considered "cosmetic". I cried when I left. I felt sick, humiliated, and sad. It no longer felt great to think of surgery. It felt embarrassing and frustrating. My issues were more than cosmetic, they were foundational, and I felt hopeless. I could not stop thinking, *why did my body not just heal from pregnancy like everyone else's?*

Maybe more is going on?

At this point, I thought surgery was the only option. I wanted a second opinion to see if another surgeon could see the *medical* needs and not just the *cosmetic* needs of my body. While waiting for another consultation, I hosted a girls' night at my home with four of my closest girlfriends. I shared with them my tummy woes. They were concerned and curious. I told them all my symptoms. Each one of them confessed, "I have all those same symptoms." Another light bulb went off. How can this be? I thought I was the only one. This cannot be normal. I could not and would not believe that this was God's design for the bodies of mothers. We could not be intended to have babies and then literally fall apart. There had to be more going on. This began my journey to learn *the truth about my core*.

The path to learning more about the true design of the *core* ultimately led to the birth of The Tummy Team.® Through my speed bumps, brokenness, desperation, and finally hope, I understood that I was not alone in this journey. God had taken every bump along the way to guide my education, my experiences, my tenacity, and my determination to help me come to a new understanding of what the *core* really is and how to help it function as He intended.[1] I no longer held my identity in sports and in the performance of my body, but my identity was now in Christ. My passion and purpose changed. My career path shifted. My girlfriends found hope in my knowledge. I understood that this journey was not just for me but for everyone who felt like me but did not have the education or clinical experience I had. It all started with fully understanding the physical design of the *core* and why a separation in that *core* is devastating to us. In the next chapter, I will share how understanding the physical design of the *core* has helped me not only heal my own *core* but to help thousands of women, men, and children experience the same.

Lessons on the Physical *Core*

WHAT IS YOUR *core*? The word has become so trendy. Working your *core* means a million different things to different people. Most of us have some preconceived idea of the *core* being a "rock-hard stomach" with six pack abs. It is something elusive, something that we all *need*, and no one has time to dedicate to developing it.

What really is your *Core*

The *core* is the center—the internal glue that holds everything else together. The *core* is not just your six pack muscles. It is all the muscles that connect your pelvis to your ribcage.

Your true *core* is comprised of the muscles that wrap around your torso and connect your upper body to your lower body. These muscles are designed to stabilize your entire body. They are designed to help support and protect your vital organs. These *core* muscles are designed to support and stabilize your spinal column. They are designed to help hold you up all day (postural muscles), help support you when you are off-balance, and help balance your body.

The health and function of your *core* is essential to the health and function of your entire body. It is not about a series of workouts or exercises. It is not about how you look in a bathing suit. It is about support, posture, power, strength, and endurance. It is more important than you know.

Anatomy of your Abdominals

After we rethink how we define the *core*, the next thing to understand is basic anatomy. It is astonishing what we can learn about how our body functions and heals when we look at how our body is designed. In PT school, we learned little about the abdominal wall. We learned a lot about the muscles in the back and the muscles of the arms and legs, but I recall next to nothing about the abdominal wall. I know we never learned about rehabilitation for the abdominal wall, and physical therapy was never ordered for someone after an abdominal surgery in the hospital.

I loved my PT school, and I believe I received a thorough education. I am not alone in this, though. Most PT's that I have worked with also admit they have little recollection of any specific abdominal education.

So, my first step to learn how to heal the *core* was to better understand the anatomy of the abdominals.

There are three distinct layers of your abdominal wall.

RECTUS ABDOMINIS

The outermost (and most superficial) layer of the abdominals is the called the *rectus abdominis*. This muscle runs from the lower rib cage straight down your middle and attaches to the pelvis and pubic bone. There is a right and a left side of this muscle, and it is connected in the center by the *linea alba*. The *rectus abdominis* is often the muscle we notice with "washboard stomachs" or "six pack" abs.

The function of this muscle is to support your organs, stabilize your back, and flex (bend forward) your torso. This muscle is the most targeted abdominal muscle with traditional abdominal exercises (sit ups, crunches, v-sits, Pilates 100, etc.).

OBLIQUES

The middle layer of the abdominal wall is called the *obliques*. The obliques run diagonally from the ribs or pelvis to the midline connective tissue (the *linea alba*). There are two sets of *obliques*—the internal *obliques* that run from the ribs to the midline and the external *obliques* that run from the pelvis to the midline.

The *obliques* function to stabilize the body, support your organs, twist your torso, side bend your torso, and flex/rotate your torso (as in a cross over crunch motion).

TRANSVERSE ABDOMINIS

The deepest layer of the abdominal wall is called your *transverse abdominis*. This muscle starts along the sides of your spine and wraps around your entire torso. It is the largest abdominal muscle.

This muscle functions like a corset or internal back brace. It stabilizes the spine, supports your organs, and brings balance and symmetry in the torso, among other benefits. This muscle is the only muscle in the entire body that has a front, back, right, and left side all within one muscle. Activation of this muscle provides symmetry and elongation in your trunk.

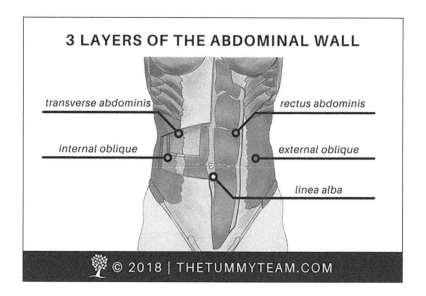

LINEA ALBA

The *linea alba* is a strip of connective tissue that runs from the pubic bone to the sternum and connects the right and left side of all three layers of the abdominal wall. The function of one layer affects the function of all three layers.

DEEP MUSCLES VERSUS SUPERFICIAL MUSCLES

The internal, deeper muscles of our body tend to be our stabilizers. These deep stabilizing muscles hold our joints together and act as postural muscles that hold us up. They are typically active in some capacity all day acting as the glue that holds us together. In the case of the abdominal wall, the *transverse abdominis* is that glue. All three layers of the abdominals act as stabilizers, but the internal corset of the *transverse abdominis* is the primary stabilizer.

Perfect Design

The complexity and beauty that is in every detail of our body is truly remarkable. Our body was designed perfectly. There is balance, coordination, and symmetry in every aspect of our body. One piece relies on another piece, and if one part of your body is injured or damaged, other parts of your body will work like crazy to help you survive and function until it is repaired.

Our body was designed for efficiency. If we just talk about muscles, it is easy to see that every muscle was designed for a specific job. In PT school, we spent several years getting an in-depth understanding of anatomy and physiology. We learned where every muscle was located, what bones it attached to, how it was meant to function in various positions, and what nerves it activates.

There is an optimal alignment and position for each muscle to function as it was designed. Many of our muscles can function in less-than-optimal alignments, but the function therefore is also less than optimal.

Disuse Atrophy

My favorite class in graduate school was neurology. Simply described, the brain communicates with every muscle in the body. It is like every muscle having a voice. The muscles that you use most have the loudest voice. The muscles you use least are more like a whisper. For example, if I asked you right now to bend your elbow and flex your bicep, you likely could do it right away. Your brain would tell your muscle to bend your elbow, and then the muscle would communicate back basically saying "look, I just bent my elbow." Now, if I told you to move your left pinky toe out and then to the side, you could likely try to tell those muscles to do that, but more than likely they would do nothing. There would be little to no movement and little to no message back saying something had happened. It would be like a phone call going unanswered.

The *transverse abdominis* is a deep muscle that has a subtle, but significant, activation with little joint movement and is often stretched out and neglected. Therefore, it has a voice of a whisper. The brain not only has a difficult time sending a signal to the transverse but often sends the wrong signal. If little to no signal is going to the transverse, the muscle does not get adequate blood flow and nerve integration. As a result, it does not build new muscle, and it inevitably stays weak.

Where Do We Begin

The first step in *core* rehabilitation is awareness. If you are unaware of the muscles you need to activate, then it is hard to activate the correct muscles. If you do not know the proper alignment that the body needs to be in to allow the corset to activate, then most of your work will be in vain. If you do not understand how your daily postures and activities affect how your body works and the muscles it recruits, then it is hard to be effective. Honestly, our lives are too full and too busy to not be effective. Understanding how your body was designed is essential to helping it *function* as it was designed.

Unfortunately, the first thing we become aware of is how weak we truly are. That knowledge can be overwhelming. We hate to feel weak. We hate to see our limitations. But there is hope! Your body was designed perfectly by God. It has an incredible capacity to heal if it is given the opportunity. Even long-standing weakness, neglect, and poor habits can be dramatically transformed with the right information and tools.

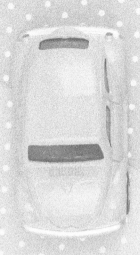

Section 2
The Spiritual *Core*

WHO'S *GOT THIS!?*

Core **Principle 1: God is sovereign.**

GOD'S CREATIVE WORK is marvelous. King David stated it best in Psalm 139:14. We are fearfully and wonderfully made!

I (Sharon) find the physical *core* to be fascinating, and I loved learning about it from Kelly. *Stability, support, the ability to turn and bend properly*—these are some of the terms Kelly used in relation to the physical *core*. It has an incredible purpose to help our body operate to its full potential. Like Kelly wrote, "The health and function of your *core* is essential to the health and function of your entire body."[1]

The concepts of *stability, support, the ability to thrive when life's bumps turn and bend us* are just as vital to our spiritual *core*. In essence, if we want to live our spiritual lives to the fullest potential, then we need to believe and *rest in* specific God-honoring principles. Let us consider the first principle—God is sovereign.

Dinosaur Controls

When my son was in kindergarten, he enjoyed playing with a particular remote-control dinosaur. It was a 'scary' tyrannosaurs rex, which came with roaring sound effects and light-up eyes. It was the type of toy where a young boy would be pleased to come suddenly behind his mother and aim to frighten her, *just for fun*.

He came to me in the kitchen one afternoon, with this treasured toy. He moved it closer and closer to me and made the dinosaur perform its scary sounds in the process. I, of course, had to *act frightened*. Then, instead of him continuing to inch the toy closer to me, he proclaimed in a sweet, yet to-the-point, voice, "Momma, DON'T be afraid of the dinosaur. I actually have the controls!"

Life can be scary for us (or at least uncomfortable). Plus, who really has the *controls*?

My son's comment struck me in a neat way. He reassured me that I did not need to fear because *he* had the controls. I immediately thought of God. He is the sovereign, creator God. He has the *controls* in our circumstances. Life may seem out of control at times, but is it *really*? We will see in this chapter that God is in control. *He* is sovereign.

The New Unger's Bible Dictionary defines the *sovereignty of God* as being the expression of the supreme rule of God. It has everything to do with God's control over His created world. I love how Unger states, "Thus understood the sovereignty of God is the great ground of confidence for his people..."[2]

Think about the word *confidence* for a moment. Confidence has to do with where we put our hope. What is the source from where we can rest easy in this chaotic world? Afterall, in this world we experience many trials and discomfort (which are out of our control). Is our confidence in self-reliance or in a streak of independence? Despite our best efforts to keep our lives under control, the bumps continue.

We miss out on peace when we fail to rest in God's strength and sovereignty. What if, deep down, we truly rested in the Scripture's teachings on the Sovereignty of God? What if we could take a step back and let God do His thing? I think we could all breathe easier if we did.

Let us consider a few specific Bible passages that clearly teach God's sovereignty in this world.

Job

I will look at the life of Job in much more detail in another chapter, but I cannot overlook the end of Job's book, especially regarding God's sovereignty. It contains one of the most exciting lists of questions in the whole Bible. These place the attention where it belongs—on God.

While Job had to work through some horrific bumps in his life, his initial response was filled with grace *and* genuine worship toward God. Throughout the book, though, we see him start to question God.

At the end of the book, Job clearly sees that God was in control of his circumstances all along. In fact, Job learned that God was distinctly in charge of His creation.

In Job 38, we read that God spoke to Job *out of the whirlwind*. Surely this grabbed Job's attention. God asked Job question after question about who was in charge. I encourage you to read Job 38-41 straight through and concentrate on the numerous ways where it clearly shows that God is sovereign.

One of God's first questions to Job was *"Where were you when I laid the foundations of the earth?" (Job 38:4)*. God continues his line of questions through Job 41.

My former graduate professor did a two-part chapel series on the book of Job. In his notes, Dr. Stephen Schrader wrote this about God's line of questions: "Eighty-three in all, none of which Job can answer! God was driving home the point that Job must let God be God, the sovereign and omnipotent Creator, who answers to no one!"[3] Schrader then stated how all of God's eighty-three questions dealt with His management and ordering of His creation.[4]

At the end of the book, Job repents of his sin of questioning God by proclaiming that no purpose of God's would be withheld (Job 42:2).

It does not get clearer than that. God is in control, and we must accept His purpose. Someone may ask, *but what about human free will? Don't I get to make choices about my life?*

I would say, yes, we do get to make choices in life. Absolutely! Yet, if God wants to bring us through a particular trial, nothing we do can stop that. We can make wise choices in life, but wise choices will not guarantee us an easy life, and that is okay. (Stay tuned for the next chapter.)

We should aim to make right choices and do everything to the glory of God (see 1 Corinthians 10:31), but our goal for these right choices should be solely to please God and not to steer clear of hardships in life. Bumps impact us all, even the "super Christian" who seemingly has everything under control. Job had to learn this.

Ecclesiastes 7:13-14

I grew up hearing my dad, Dr. Gregory Christopher, preach on this scripture. I have notes written in my Bible under this section, and it has always been an encouraging go-to passage when I need to refresh my mind about God's control in difficult circumstances.

"Consider the work of God; For who can make straight what He has made crooked? In the day of prosperity be joyful, but in the day of adversity consider: Surely God has appointed the one as well as the other, so that man can find out nothing that will come after him" (Eccles. 7:13-14).

We may get frustrated about what God "has bent" in our lives. Perhaps we want some situation "straightened out" in our timing. This is not how God works, though.[5]

Let us briefly look at the word *consider*. In our passage, this word occurs twice, and it is the same Hebrew word both times. The term carries the idea of *to reflect on*. The *Complete Word Study Bible* shows that this verb requires a person to make a mental observation and for

27

the person to see outside of himself.[6] In essence, the term, *consider*, shows that the world does not revolve around us.

Sometimes God provides us with a life of ease. Praise God and be joyful. Yet, when times get difficult, we have an opportunity to consider God's hand at work. Did you catch how verse 14 says that God is the one *appointing* the two options: prosperity or adversity?

God brings about a variety of life circumstances so that we realize that we are not God, AND we are not the one in charge. We are not promised to see what is headed our way on our life's *road*. What an interesting concept to ponder.

Ecclesiastes further shows that life can sometimes be quite unfair. In our eyes, we see how good things happen to bad people or think they have it easy. (See Eccles. 7:15 and 8:14.)

Why must humans have such bumpy roads in life? Do you find yourself more easily frustrated when experiencing life's bumpy roads? Here are some questions you may ask. Why does this person get the quick line in the grocery store? Does God not know that *I* need to get home first? Why does my loud obnoxious neighbor have such a nice boat in his driveway, and *I* do not even have the means to go enjoy the lake? Why does she get such good grades, while hardly studying, and *I* had to pull an all-nighter just to pass? Why does that family get to travel, and *I* never go anywhere? *I* do not deserve this...I...I...I...and the list could go on and on. Does this sound familiar?

When our life gets too *bendy* for our liking, we must remember that God is the One in control. Our job is to respect (trust and obey)

God's way. This is our duty and is precisely the way that Ecclesiastes ends. (See Eccles. 12:13.)

<u>A Historical Application of Ecclesiastes 7</u>

In one of my children's Social Studies' lessons, they were learning about the Pilgrims' voyage on the Mayflower. Their BJU Press text-book mentions, "On a cold November day, an English ship reached the New World. The *Mayflower* had been blown and tossed at sea. The sailors planned to land just north of Jamestown. But storms carried the ship much farther north. God had brought the *Mayflower* to the northeast coast of America."[7]

They *planned* to sail and land near Jamestown, but a *storm* changed things for them. Some may say this was chance or fate. Based on Ecclesiastes, these are inaccurate thoughts.

The history lesson then covered this verse:

"Whatever the LORD pleases He does, In heaven and in earth, In the seas and in all deep places" (Ps. 135:6).

What a testament to God's sovereignty. He absolutely had the role in where the Pilgrims landed. That storm was no surprise for Him. This same concept still holds true.

Chapter's Concluding Thoughts

We cannot delve more fully into this book without first clearly noting the sovereign God that we serve. This chapter's key principle, mixed with the next chapter's principle, will lay the groundwork for *how* we need to respond to the hard bumps that we are guaranteed to go through in life.

Before going further in this book, I encourage you to pray and ask God to soften your heart, if necessary, and be encouraged that HE is in control—even when life gets a little *too bumpy*.

For further study, here are some additional verses on the topic of God's sovereignty.

- **1 Samuel 14:6b**

When King Saul's son, Jonathan, went to battle with the Philistine army, he told his armor bearer, "For nothing restrains the LORD from saving by many or by few."

- **1 Chronicles 29:10-12**

David began singing praises to God (verse 10), and David states God reigns over all (verse 12).

- **Job 9:4, 12**

Job declares that God is wise and mighty (verse 4), and Job states that nobody can hinder God (verse 12).

- **Psalm 83:18**

Asaph declares that the LORD is the "Most High" over this earth.

- **Psalm 97:1-2**

God's sovereign rule is taught in this chapter. Since God reigns, we can rejoice!

- **Psalm 104**

This whole chapter is a beautiful picture of God's sovereignty. If you ever need a *pick-me-up* spiritually, this Psalm is neat and encouraging, and it contains vivid word pictures of His rule over the earth.

- **Psalm 135:6**

God's sovereign rule is also clearly taught in this verse. God will accomplish that which He pleases.

- **Proverbs 16:9**

King Solomon wrote that God is the one directing man's steps.

- **Isaiah 43:13**

God is speaking in this verse and states that nobody will be able to reverse what God chooses to do.

- **Daniel 4:34-37**

After the rise and then humiliation of King Nebuchadnezzar, he honored God and proclaimed God's dominion and command over inhabitants of the earth. He ends his speech by admitting his own downfall and how God can humble man.

Application Thoughts for Chapter 3

1. In what way(s) has it been difficult to let God have the *controls* in your life?

2. Is there an area in your life where you lack confidence in God's workings?

3. What specific sovereignty passage(s) can you dwell on during your *bumps*?

4. In Job 38-41, what are your favorite questions that God presents to Job? Specifically, which question(s) positively challenges you the most, and why?

5. I encourage you to pray and ask God to soften any areas of your heart where you may struggle to hand over control to Him.

The Difficult Days

Core Principle 2: Trials have purpose.

I CAME ACROSS a Facebook post, written by Angie Chance. Her daughter, Desirae Howell, and I were high school friends. I could not help but giggle *and* cringe (on Angie's behalf) when I saw this post. I tried to put myself in her shoes. What a stressful day!

My Day:

Mitch spilled scalding hot tea on my leg first thing this morning! Then, as I'm in the shower [he] tells me he's going to burn trash! Then after blow drying my hair...I notice the yard is on fire, and Mitch is gone, and the brush in the woods are glowing nicely, as well! I grab minimal clothes and shoes and my phone and a shovel. I text Mitch...'yard on fire' and proceed to beat the burning leaves and grass with a shovel.

Meanwhile the cute little fire is spreading. So I stop beating and just start using the shovel as a rake. Then I manage to inhale a burning cinder. (Mitch might have been called a few unsavory, but well-deserved names). Finally a neighbor shows up to help, but I've pretty much got it under control. Then Austin Chance showed up and took momma's shovel and double checked my burn piles. Thank you neighbor and Austin. Tonight, Mitch proceeds to hug me (I had to make him because I'm coughing and the hypochondriac is afraid of me). He says 'mmmmm you smell like BBQ!' I need help hiding the body.[1]

Life is full of interesting moments. I am sure Angie did not wake up that day and expect such jolting experiences. Her cortisol levels were probably a little higher than usual. Though Angie's story was worthy of a Facebook post, it proves that life is filled with uncertainty.

We must keep the previous chapter in mind when we work through this chapter. A sovereign God brings trials into our lives—BUT—they serve a purpose. This chapter's principle is what brings us encouragement *in our bumps.*

Much is said in the Bible about *difficult days.* I really want to highlight three particular passages.

Romans 8

Perhaps the middle of Romans 8 can be our guidepost when dealing with bumps in life. The chapter has us considering our sufferings (Rom. 8:18). Bumps will come along the way. We see that sometimes our weaknesses in life are so big that we do not even know how to pray amid such trials (Rom. 8:26). Praise God, though, because His Holy Spirit is making intercession for us...all the way to the throne of God (Rom. 8:26-27).

This leads us to one of the neatest set of verses in the Bible (verses 28-29). Believers are promised that all our life's circumstances, including our trials, work for our good. It does not mean that our trials make us *feel* good. It means that our bumps serve a spiritual purpose in our lives. Specifically, these trials are so that we can become more like Christ (Rom. 8:29). We will not grow spiritually without trials. Without trials, our faith will not be stretched. It really comes down to perspective. Do we view our trials through the correct lens? Do we view our bumps as the means to become more Christlike? Do we increase our faith or let the bumps squelch our trust in God? Whether we like it or not, trials are designed for our good.

We must remember that for the Christian, *all things* work together for good (Rom. 8:28). Biblical Counselor, Rosalie Francetich, compares this phrase (*all things*) to both a sieve and a window screen.[2] A sieve or a window screen allows <u>some</u> things in (or out) but not <u>everything</u>. Rosalie says that God only allows things in our lives that He will use to make us more Christlike. God has 'coursework' designed specifically for us to grow us and increase our faith. She encourages others to think about the <u>response</u> when trials are allowed to pass through.[3] It really comes down to proper perspective.

James 1:2-4

"My brethren, count it all joy when you fall into various trials, knowing that the testing of your faith produces patience. But let patience have its perfect work, that you may be perfect and complete, lacking nothing" (James 1:2-4).

When a trial strikes, what is our first response? Do we *count it as joy*? In the initial moments, when I am *bumped,* I sometimes exhibit more frustration and internal grumbling than joy. It can take me time to step aside and think through what the Bible teaches on this topic.

So, what does James mean when he said to "count it all joy" when you are in a trial? Another of my former professors, Dr. Kevin Carson, said this about when we are in the *thick of things*: "Joy grows out of reasoned evaluation. Rather than reckless emotion, you stop, think, and evaluate. You know what God is doing in the circumstance and know the mercy and comfort of God. So, you can reason that the circumstance is a joy-filled circumstance".[4]

We are not being asked to rejoice *over* the pain. We are not required to say: *yay, yay, yay, we are in the midst of pain*! We can, however, rejoice over the *effects*. We can rejoice in the *result*, which is spiritual growth.

Specifically, how are trials designed to grow us? The testing of our faith produces patience (verse 3). This term carries the idea of endurance. Carson states that, "Endurance looks like developing permanent inner strength. We have to consider the big picture. The goal is not to get out of the circumstance, the goal is to be godly through it."[5]

What do *perfect* and *complete* mean in this passage? They do not mean perfection in the way we view it today. They carry the idea of spiritual maturity. Carson states that, "Various circumstances are God's way of allowing us to gain that which we are lacking. God adapts trials to our character to provide what we need! It is not always what we want or what we think we need."[6]

Words from an Endurance Runner

It was fascinating to speak with Brad Williams, an endurance runner. He has completed eleven marathons, including the Boston

Marathon on two occasions. In each race, Brad was able to improve his finish time with a new personal record.

Brad spoke about the intensity that his body went through to be prepared for races. In the early days, his muscles would be very strained, his body exhausted and worn. He spoke of the "total misery" his body felt, but he kept moving toward his goal to initially qualify for Boston and then chase the elusive sub-three-hour finish time before moving on to competing in Ironman Triathlons.

As an endurance runner, Brad had to improve in both speed and endurance. It was a discipline, he said. He could not just skip training when he did not feel like working hard. He wanted to *train right*.

He mentioned the purpose for straining his body. Yes, he was motivated to finish his races well. He wanted to improve each time. It was imperative, though, that he do his best to get his body *race ready*. For him, keeping this in mind helped him continue to train, even when it was hard. The resulting muscle pain allowed his muscles to strengthen. Pushing hard brought soreness, but he knew that once the muscles repaired, they would be *stronger*.[7]

A successful runner must put his body through much physical stress. In similar fashion, God knows what we need to help grow us spiritually. If we were never spiritually stretched from trials (from the loving hand of God), how would we really learn to trust God and increase in spiritual maturity? Our spiritual muscles would not grow. In fact, they would shrivel.

A Scenario

Pretend you are excited to go on a picnic with your family. Your local meteorologist said the afternoon would be lovely—no rain, a light breeze, and mild humidity. You set out your picnic spread, and position everyone in their cutest clothes so that you could get a group picture during this grandly-planned picnic. Suddenly, dark clouds enter. It starts to pour. Everyone screams and runs for cover.

Perhaps you say some *choice* words under your breath, or you get angry that your day is ruined. What if your family sees an unpretty response? Hmmmmm...what happened? Life happened; that is for sure.

There was certainly room for one of two options—a proper or improper response. I do not know why God causes weather to sometimes "crash our fun." I do know that if we needed additional practice in contentment, exhibiting proper speech, or—fill in the blank—that if we trusted God's sovereign plan instead of getting mad, that we would be taking a step toward Christian growth instead of having an improper response.

I get it. It is easier said than done. However, I think I could *practice* better faith-filled responses. Proper practice in the smaller trials sets us up for a more God-honoring response when bigger trials hit.

Lemon Example

Lemons...How are they useful? Some of you like to make lemonade or enjoy them in your water. Some may use the zest for a recipe, while others use lemons in science experiments to counteract with baking soda!

Carol Stock Kranowitz wrote a book for children with sensory needs, called *The Out-of-Sync Child Has Fun*. She includes a neat idea for a 'press and squeeze' lemon activity. You hold a lemon with the purpose of squeezing it with your hand or foot. You can press on the lemon firmly and roll it back and forth.[8] I have done a similar activity with my children. I let them throw lemons on the garage floor and chase them.

Kranowitz states that, "Rather than damage the fruit, the pressure actually improves it by breaking down the pulp to yield more juice."[9] This illustration goes right along with James 1. Amid a trial, I must ask myself: *how is my attitude when I am squeezed and pressed and thrown about by life's trials? Do I have the right perspective?* I do not always think long-term about the spiritual fruit I could bear by having proper responses.

What is the *better way*? Afterall, trials are a guarantee. Are we wasting the trial by grumbling through it? Are we allowing the trial to cloud our thinking that we forget God is up to something good?

1 Peter 1:6-7a

"In this you greatly rejoice, though now for a little while, if need be, you have been grieved by various trials, that the genuineness of your faith, being much more precious than gold that perishes..."(1 Pet. 1:6-7a).

I have always appreciated the writings of the late Warren Wiersbe. He was known as the "Pastor's Pastor." I like how he practically divided up these two verses:

- "Trials meet needs." (This covers the idea of "if need be" in the passage.)

- "Trials are varied."

- "Trials are not easy."

- "Trials are controlled by God."[10]

This passage teaches that trials (though difficult) are still useful. Our faith can be proven to be genuine when we go through some bump *and* respond well. Mistakes will happen, though. For encouragement, please consider the illustration below.

<u>Broken Glass</u>

What if (either currently or in the past) you broke under the pressure of some trial? What if you shattered some piece(s) of your life when a trial swept you off your feet?

Here is an illustration from Pastor Robert A. Carlson. Broken glass can be dangerous. Like glass, we can seem broken at times. We may have jagged edges, and we may hurt others as a result. We may think that nothing good can come out of our mess and ruin. Something new *can* be made from the brokenness, though. God can turn something that is seemingly destroyed into something beautiful.[11]

Below is a set of pictures showing this illustration. While the first shows broken glass, the second shows a glass giraffe. Carlson (and his wife, Julie) own many glass-made animals from Africa. Each was made from **recycled glass**.[12]

God can fix us in our broken state(s)! He offers guaranteed forgiveness (see 1 John 1:9) and can renew us daily.

The prophet Jeremiah wrote a stunning portrayal of God's faithfulness and goodness! When his soul was sinking, Jeremiah had to bring something *particular* to the forefront of his mind. Jeremiah stated how he had to believe that God's mercies were refreshed each day; therefore, Jeremiah could place his hope in God's faithfulness (See Lam. 3:22-24).

Chapter's Concluding Thoughts

We must maintain a heavenly perspective on the *purpose* of trials. God wants to facilitate spiritual growth in our lives. He is not some mean Heavenly Father that always requires evil against us. No, quite the opposite is true. He wants to provide precise opportunities to allow us to mature in our faith. Our loving God does not leave us to helplessly falter in our faith. He gives us chances to be stretched, yet solely for our good.

Wiersbe put it this way: "If we value comfort more than character, then trials will upset us. If we value the material and physical more than the spiritual, we will not be able to "count it all joy." If we live only for the present and forget the future, then trials will make us bitter, not better."[13] I pray that we do not waste the bumps!

Application Thoughts for Chapter 4

1. What *bumps* in your life are particularly difficult to have pass through your *window screen* or *sieve*?

2. What do you think is your primary, or first, go-to response when a trial strikes? Do you consistently *consider it joy*?

3. Try to spend time dwelling on James 1:2-4. Take note of how God may be wanting to work in your heart in this area.

4. Analyze your spiritual "muscles" in hardships. Are you increasing in your spiritual stamina?

5. How is your overall perspective when *squeezed* by pressures of life? Are you thinking long-term (spiritual growth) or short-term (a desire for immediate comfort)?

6. If you feel you have been broken into pieces of glass (because of some trial overtaking you), ask God to restore you. You are still useable!

Resultant Faith

Core **Principle 3: Our faith must stay rooted in God.**

MY CHILDREN WERE watching a new episode of PAW
Patrol during the 2020 election cycle. It was a timely episode, as
there was a mayoral race going on in *Adventure Bay*. Would the *evil*
Mayor Humdinger win? Would he get more votes than Adventure
Bay's current, beloved Mayor Goodway?[1]

My young son was really involved in this episode. He was jumping
up and down cheering for the good mayor. He kept loudly proclaiming how he hoped Mayor Goodway would win. My sweet and
slightly older daughter logically kept trying to assure of him of the
obvious impending outcome. "Of course Mayor Goodway will win,"
she said! If you have watched PAW Patrol, you would agree that
there was *no way* Humdinger would win in the end.

My daughter was rightly assured of the obvious victory. We, too,
can be rightly assured of God's promises in His Word. The previous
two chapters covered God's sovereignty and His purpose for trials.
We can be assured that we have the spiritual victory *in Him*. This, of
course, does not mean we will never struggle in our faith. In future
chapters, I will walk through how to practically deal with struggles

in our faith. Yet, if we really hold to the principles of God being in control *and* having a purpose for trials, we can have resultant faith that we *can* come through trials on the positive side.

Math Facts

I am not particularly good with math facts. I do know, though, that in addition, switching the <u>order</u> of the addends does not change the answer. In the below math equation, the order of *core* principles 1 and 2 does not matter. The importance is that both addends need to be followed consistently, even if they are switched, to come to the correct answer.

One's full belief in:

Core Principle 1 (God is sovereign) + *Core* Principle 2 (Trials have purpose) = *Core* Principle 3 (Our faith must stay rooted in God)

If we believe that God is in control, yet do not believe that any good comes from trials, then the above math equation will not get us to the answer of *faith*. On the other hand, if we believe that trials do have some purpose but do not believe that God is all-sovereign and knows what He is doing, then we will still not be confident in God's plan. It is essential that we believe *core* principles 1 and 2 so that we have proper faith in God.

Life gets hectic, and sometimes (or maybe oftentimes) we fail in our faith. Please allow me to take a moment to address a common phrase, "just have faith". This phrase leads to understandable frustration as one attempts to put a finger on this seemingly obscure concept. I think the following explanation from Kevin Carson will help ease this frustration. We may have the ***head*** *knowledge* about what we should believe about God. Do we have the ***hand*** *knowledge*, though? This is where there is behavioral change.[2]

This is where the rubber meets the road. This is where faith comes into play. In our personal lives, are we willing and ready to consider God's sovereign ways AND have confidence in His plans? Do we have deep-down faith in His plans for our lives? If we do not, trials will do more than just shake us. They could destroy us. If we do exhibit faith, trials will grow us and bring us closer to Christ. This *core* concept about faith is *that* big of a deal!

A Sermon on Faith

I would like to walk you through a sermon by Pastor Phillip Housley. In March 2020, I listened to his sermon online, just as the nationwide shutdown was happening due to COVID-19. It was a timely sermon about faith during scary times. It was entitled *A Day in the Life of Jesus*.[3] Housley dissected Matthew 8:24-27.

These verses in Matthew 8 follow Jesus's Sermon on the Mount. Jesus experienced a series of busy events leading up to 8:24-27. Jesus was bombarded with a grueling schedule.

- Jesus healed a leper (Matt. 8:2-3).

- Jesus entered Capernaum and healed a centurion's servant (Matt. 8:5-7).

- Jesus healed Peter's mother-in-law (Matt. 8:14-15).

- At evening time, Jesus cast out demons (Matt. 8:16).

- Jesus and His disciples entered a boat (Matt. 8:23).

Suddenly, a great storm arose while Jesus and the disciples were on this boat. Housley then went through events that transpired from the storm. It was such a major storm that the ship was covered with waves (Matt. 8:24). There was hopelessness. Jesus's disciples came to him, woke Him, and proclaimed how they were about to perish (Matt. 8:25).

In essence, Jesus then asked the disciples, "Where is your faith!?" Did the disciples not remember *all* the miracles Jesus had just done? We may think, *how did they have such weak faith at that point in time*?

Jesus calmed the storm for his disciples. Yet, the disciples had to learn an important lesson (Matt. 8:27). They had to personally acknowledge Christ's authority and power. How quickly do we 'catch on' to exercise faith?

Housley then stated that, "Jesus was there in the midst of that mess. Don't allow the existence of problems cause you to think God is not present. Jesus wanted them to have faith in Him."[4] It is our responsibility to live out that faith.

Pardon the pun, but we are all in the same boat, right? I have seen God's workings in my life numerous times, but I know I am guilty of lacking faith at times. The disciples feared the storm. Here are some things that we may fear:

- Financial woes

- Health problems

- Danger for our children

- Family issues

- The unknown

It is important for us to remember what the disciples had to learn (the hard way) on that stormy day: in our life's storm, God is still in control and can be trusted. Especially when times get tough, we need to rest in these same principles.

When Our Faith Is Lacking

When my son was a baby, I would internally giggle if I heard the hymn, *Because He Lives*.[5] The song goes "Because He lives, I can face tomorrow..." The song's emphasis is since Jesus is alive, we have the strength to face our tomorrows. I told myself, *forget the tomorrow part...I need help TODAY!* Have you experienced some trial in life that made each day stretch into what felt like an eternity?

Let us be honest with ourselves. There are times when our faith is lacking, yet we do not desire this to be so. What can we do to "pull up our bootstraps" for an improved attitude?

Christians have a key player to help us keep our faith in our spiritual battles. In 1 Thessalonians 1:1-7, the Apostle Paul was thanking the church in Thessalonica for their work of *faith* (among other things). They had received the Gospel in much *affliction* (1:6). Yet, they received this Truth with *joy of the Holy Spirit* (1:6b). Walvoord and Zuck emphasize the driving force of the Thessalonians' joy: "The source of their joy was the indwelling Holy Spirit."[6] The Holy Spirit can take the Word of God and help us maintain our faith, even when it is difficult.

Paul writes a second letter to the church in Thessalonica. He again commends them for their growing *faith* (2 Thessalonians 1:3). Their faith did not just grow while they were in easy times. These Christians experienced persecution and tribulation (2 Thess. 1:4) while growing their faith!

If these believers could increase faith in scary times, so can we! We serve the same powerful God.

Sacrifice of Praise

When thinking through these *pesky bumps* in life, it is easy to lose heart. When our faith is minimal, an attitude of praise and thanksgiving become a must. When we find our faith shrinking, we must turn our focus to God. If we keep the focus on the trial at hand, there is no way we will keep a proper attitude. I believe a turning point in our faith is when we can genuinely **choose** to offer thanksgiving and praise to God, <u>no matter what is at hand</u>.

For me, Hebrews 13:15 was one of the main Bible verses that spurred me to keep faith when my children were young, and life was stressful.

"Therefore, by Him let us continually offer the sacrifice of praise to God, that is, the fruit of our lips, giving thanks to his name" (Heb. 13:15).

This verse is short, but it packs a punch. Let us first, briefly, consider it in context with the rest of the book of Hebrews. The context will help bring appreciation to the idea of *sacrifice*.

There is a major difference between the Old Testament Jewish sacrificial system and the Church Age. In *The Complete Word Study Dictionary*, Zodhiates writes, "The Levitical sacrifices were perpetually repeated because they had no permanent efficacy. Christ's sacrifice is made once for all...The basic purpose of the writer of the Epistle to the Hebrews is to mark the radical difference between the Christian and the Levitical concepts of sacrifice."[7]

I cannot help but feel a little badly for the early church-age Christians, especially the Jewish believers in Jesus. There was a substantial shift that took place once Jesus died on the cross. There was surely some confusion about what was or was not expected of them regarding sacrifices. I think our main verse (Hebrews 13:15) would have been a true help to the early church regarding the sacrificial transition.

Praise God, Old Testament sacrifices are now unnecessary, but we are not *off the hook*. Our sacrifice is different now, but it does not mean it is always easy. We learn in the New Testament that we are to be *living sacrifices* for God (Romans 12:1). The Greek word for *sacrifice* in Romans 12:1 is the same Greek word for *sacrifice* in Hebrews 13:15.

Let us look at the term *sacrifice*. It is the act of offering. Sure, we know the word, but do we *do* the word enough? I think of a child who is struggling to share a particular toy. If a parent *makes* him share, the child is not offering up the toy. On the other hand, if the child willingly hands over a toy, he truly *offers* it to his friend. This is really a *sacrificial* act.

In our verse, what are we supposed to be sacrificing or willingly offering up to God? We are to offer up a sacrifice of praise to God.

Why is this such an interesting or profound concept? Isn't it always EASY to praise God? Unfortunately, no.

It comes down to this: our spiritual sacrifice is continual praise to God, no matter the size or frequency of the bump.

Take a moment to think through a life event(s) that made it difficult for you to sacrificially praise God. Was it a recent event? Is it a current event through which you are struggling?

Sacrifice of Praise...Find a Way!

Unfortunately, there are no *"what if* or *but"* clauses in Hebrews 13:15. This is where the act of sacrifice comes in to play.

It is not an option for us to ponder if any given trial is *worthy-enough* to praise God over or not. We are commanded to praise, regardless of the trial.

One of my favorite quotes comes from Elizabeth George, in *A Woman's Walk With God.* She writes, "Although I don't *feel* like praising the Lord or thanking Him, I *do* what God says, and that effort makes my praise a sacrifice."[8] George heavily influenced my thinking on this idea of "Sacrifice of Praise."

My favorite part of her quote is the idea of **effort.** When we are knee-deep (maybe even neck-deep) in a trial, the effort we put forth to praise God (even when we absolutely do not feel like it), is really a sacrifice. While in our fleshly hot mess, when we least feel like praising God, it is precisely the time to make the effort to praise Him. Then, we can be sure we have offered a sacrifice up to God with the fruit of our lips. "Through the power of the Holy Spirit, this act of thanksgiving transforms our pain into praise."[9]

Example of Robert Hunt

Here is another example from my children's history book. It is from an excerpt on Robert Hunt. He came to Jamestown in 1607 so that he could be a pastor to the Native Americans in that area. He wound up becoming a preacher to the men in Jamestown.

Here is an example of Hunt trusting God during a trial. The textbook states, "He did not complain, even when a fire in the fort burned up his books."[10] For a preacher to lose books in such a way—and in that day and age—would be difficult! What an incredible attitude to not become angry or bitter about such a loss.

Chapter's Concluding Thoughts

The main point is, we must keep our focus on God and His character and promises, not on ourselves and our hardships. Remember God sovereignly brings trials for a purpose. Our part is to maintain faith.

We may be in awe of a Biblical concept, such as a *sacrifice of praise*, but our awe does not automatically equate to application. In the depths of our tiredness, or in the middle of another crazy day, you and I must battle our thoughts so that we do not say or think, "*God, why are you doing this to me!?*" Or "*God, I CANNOT handle this; take it from me now.*" It takes real effort for us to praise God in the middle of a truly awful day.

We all have our own versions of fleshly battles of questioning or wondering why a particular trial will not ease up. Fighting the flesh is exhausting, but if we make a practice of making the *effort* to praise God, then it will become more natural to allow praise to become the habit of our heart. Let us find a way to sacrifice our praise.

Application Thoughts for Chapter 5

1. In the chapter's beginning "math fact equation", is there a particularly difficult part to stay focused on in relation to trials?

2. Is there an area of your life where you can give your fears (or frustrations) over to God? I encourage you to take time to pray about this now.

3. Think through past examples where God has brought you through a life difficulty. Dwell on His *track record* of faithfulness. How can this help you through a current *bump*?

4. What is your personal, fleshly battle where it can be a struggle to praise God? For example, is it harder to praise God when you are tired, stressed, overworked, etc?

5. In what ways can you plan—and choose—to make the extra **effort** to offer the sacrifice of praise to God?

"Woah, God" vs. "Okay, God"

Consider these scenarios:

SALLY WAS ON her way to her best friend's wedding when her back tire blew out in her new SUV. She was pulled over to the side of her country road for two hours while waiting for the tow truck. Not only did she miss the wedding, but she missed the throwing of the bouquet at the reception. She and her friend had even concocted a plan to have Sally catch it. Sally bemoaned her awful day and said, "<u>Woah God</u>, not fair!"

Mayley was guaranteed a promotion at her job that she has faithfully been working at for the past five years. Then, she came in to work one Monday morning to see a new face sitting at her promised desk in the office nearby. It was a younger face than her own. What happened? Mayley, for some unknown reason, lost out on the promotion. Her coworkers knew it was not fair, and they offered their opinions about it openly to Mayley. Mayley thought quietly about everything once everyone left her office, and she said, "<u>Okay, God</u>, I will trust You."

Though these specific trials may not be our own, there is one factor that will match our real-life situations. It is the fact that we are guaranteed to have a RESPONSE to the trial. Will our response to annoyances be like Sally's *"Woah, God"* or like Mayley's *"Okay, God?"*

I have been recently guilty of *"Woah, God"* after my car accident with my children, in that I was unhappy about the inconvenience it placed on my children and me. With all our medical appointments and rushed schedules, I just *knew* that we could not get in another crash again! Rosalie Francetich, really helped me to get back on track with trusting God's plan for my life. Lord-willing, next time, I will not take so long for a God-honoring response!

In this chapter, we will consider two possible heart responses to bumps on our road: *"Woah, God"* or *"Okay, God."* We will look at Biblical examples of how these concepts play out in 'real life'. Let us specifically consider the lives of Job, Naomi, Paul, and Jesus.

Job

Stephen Schrader preached on the book of Job in two separate graduate school chapels. He was noticeably passionate about the book and how the details played out. His excitement for the book rubbed off on me. Here is what Schrader said about the purpose of the book of Job: "It is to show that the proper relationship between God and man is based solely on the sovereign grace of God and man's response of faith and submissive trust."[1] The book of Job carries the idea of having submissive trust by faith.

I will break up Job's materials into five sections to help keep things organized.

Section 1: Two Scenes: Heaven and Earth

Let us look at specific verses that speak to Job's integrity. He was upright in behavior, feared God, and shunned evil (Job 1:1). Similar adjectives were used of Job again (1:8). When Satan came before the presence of God (and was up to no good), God had Satan consider his servant, Job. Job was a godly man. Yet, Job was unaware of this *meeting* happening in heaven. Satan was convinced that if Job experienced pain and loss of riches, that Job would then curse God. God sovereignly allowed Satan to bring about havoc in Job's life to show Job's life as a testament of faith, despite his circumstances.

Havoc and deep pain did strike. In quick fashion, Job had livestock stolen and servants killed (Job 1:14-15), a fire struck causing more animals and servants to be killed (Job 1:16), camels were stolen and more servants killed (Job 1:17), and his children died (Job 1:18-19). This is more intense than one can imagine!

Job's response, though, was one of trust. It was as if he said in his heart, "*Okay, God!*" Here is his response:

Then Job arose, tore his robe, and shaved his head; and he fell to the ground and worshipped. And he said: "Naked I came from my mother's womb, and naked shall I return there. The LORD gave, and the LORD has taken away; Blessed be the name of the LORD" (Job 1:20-21).

In their commentary, Editors Walvoord and Zuck wrote that a torn robe symbolizes inner turmoil and shock. They mention that falling to the ground shows worship and not despair. In this rapid loss, Job praised God.[2]

The next verse is just as powerful. It tells us that Job did not charge God with wrong. He did not fight God and His plan. In the next chapter in Job, God again tells Satan that Job was still upright and honorable before God (Job 2:3). Job's trials did not end there, though. He was struck with boils from head to toe. When his wife tried to get him to curse God, Job refused. He knew that he could accept either good or adversity from the hand of God (Job 2:10).

His response of faith amazes me. Satan was proven wrong. Job did not curse God in adversity; he trusted. There is more to the story that we should consider, though. Will Job keep his response of *"Okay, God?"*

Section 2: Job's Friends Enter the Scene

Job's friends enter the scene and have a week of silence with him (Job 2:11-13). Then, they offer him some not-so-friendly 'encouragement' filled with wrong assumptions.

- Eliphaz tells Job he is reaping punishment because of some wrongdoing (Job 4:7-8).

- Zophar told Job to get rid of iniquity and wickedness (Job 11:14).

- Eliphaz said Job's wickedness is great and his iniquities are without end (Job 22:5).

- Job calls his friends out as miserable comforters (Job 16:1-2).

- Job declares he wants to hold fast to his righteousness. Remember how Job was described at the start of the book. He had integrity (Job 27:5-6).

- God calls the friends out for wrong speaking (Job 42:7).

Poor Job, I feel for him. What a confusing, trial-filled time.

<u>Section 3: Job Starts to 'Switch Gears'</u>

Unfortunately, we do see moments of *"Woah, God"* sprinkled throughout the book.

- Job argues it was God who has afflicted him (Job 6:4).

- Job wants to reason with God (Job 9:1-4).

- Job wants a chance to plead with God for justice's sake (Job 9:19).

- He wishes he could go to court with God if God were a man (Job 9:32).

- Job states, "Show me why You contend with me" (Job 10:1-2).

- Job declares he wants to reason with God (Job 13:1-3).

- He wants to argue before God and plead his case (Job 23-1:7).

- He wants God to answer him (Job 31:35).

Schrader states, "The Book of Job extensively employs legal terms and metaphors in the process of its dialogue concerning the disputed innocence of Job before God."[3] Job started to make demands and called on God as if to take Him to court.

Section 4: God's Response

Get ready for it, Job (and us)!

Then the LORD answered Job out of the whirlwind...Now prepare yourself like a man; I will question you, and you shall answer Me" (Job 38:1a, 3).

God turned the tables in a neatly dramatic fashion. In chapters 38-41, God presented question after question about God's magnificent management of His ordering of creation.[4] God was clearly the One who had control over the world (and life's circumstances)! Midway through these questions, Job answered that he was vile and did not know how to respond (Job 40:4-5).

Section 5: Job's Final Reply

At the end of the book, we see real heart change in Job's response. He submitted to God's plan in the end. He repented and wanted to change the direction of wrongful questioning of God's ways. He wanted to turn things back over to the sovereign God (Job 42:1-6). The book ends on a good note, with Job again learning to say *Okay God*.

Naomi

In the book of Ruth, we see a family trial right away. In this Old Testament book, we are introduced to husband and wife, Elimelech and Naomi, who lived in Bethlehem. There was famine in the land; so they and their two sons moved to Moab. While there, Elimelech died. Naomi's two sons married Moabite women (Orpah and Ruth), but the sons later died.

As the story proceeds, we learn that daughter-in-law, Ruth, returns to Bethlehem with Naomi. When back home, the townspeople were excited to see Naomi again (Ruth 1:19). Naomi was quick to tell these people that she wanted to be called "Mara", meaning bitter. She stated how God had dealt bitterly in her life. She spoke of God's affliction and sounded mad about how God brought her back home empty. It sounds more like *"Woah, God"* in her response.

Fast forward to later in the book. We see Ruth marry a man named Boaz, and they get pregnant (Ruth 4:13). Naomi was told that her grandson would restore her life and nourish her in her old age (Ruth 4:15).

I had never considered the following until our former Sunday School teacher, Matt Vanderford, spoke on this very topic.[5]

Would the only thing that could change Naomi's attitude be a more *positive* set of circumstances? I am certainly not being harsh or judgmental with her. She was a grieving widow who also lost both of her sons. But no matter the circumstances, many of us may still struggle to have faith and joy in our own situations. Times are tough, we complain. Something does not go our way, we get frustrated. Things get better, and only then, we take a sigh of relief and our demeanor changes. Where is our faith and trust all along?

The Apostle Paul

I like the Apostle Paul. He is a self-professed 'learner of contentment' and was able to live a life of "*Okay, God.*" Before we see this through to fruition, let us briefly consider Paul's life, pre-salvation. Paul's upbringing seemed well to-do. He was trained under an excellent instructor, Gamaliel (Acts 22:3). This would have been a major privilege.

We see Paul in a negative light in Acts 7. This is when he (then called 'Saul') was involved in the martyrdom of Stephen. The ones committing the act of stoning laid their garments at the feet of Saul (Acts 7:58).

Why in the world do I even delve into the pre-saved life of Paul? Who cares about his upbringing and leadership role in such a bad group? There is no reason to even discuss a "*Woah, God*" vs."*Okay, God*" scenario in the life of an unbeliever, right!?

Wrong. Here is why I bring it up. He had a great education and was well-known. He had 'pull' and was a leader with people under his leadership. Then, he gets saved, which is amazing, but it also meant he had a change in his life's role. He went from being a leader to the one being chased out of town at times. (See Acts 14.) Here is the kicker, and he states it best himself: he had to LEARN contentment. (See Phil. 4:11.)

What is the backdrop to learning contentment? Let us just consider the end of the book of Acts. For starters, Paul was arrested by an angry mob (Acts 21:26-36). There was an uproar among the Jewish people, and they wanted to kill Paul because they did not like the truth that he was preaching. He was going to be taken to trial. Amid this chaos, more than forty men formed a pact that they would not eat or drink until they could kill Paul (Acts 23:12-13). Jewish leaders wanted Paul to come back to Jerusalem to ambush him (Acts 25:1-4). These same people were then invited to go along on the journey and accuse Paul officially. What!? Things were not going to be getting any better for Paul any time soon.

In Caesarea, he came before the judgement seat. Serious accusations and complaints were made that were not even provable (Acts 25:6-8). Paul would be sent to Rome to appeal to Caesar. On his way, he was in a shipwreck (Acts 27:39ff). Once back on solid ground, a snake bit him (Acts 28:3). To end the dramatic set of events, Paul was put under house arrest for two years (Acts 28). Just typing all of that was stressful for me! I cannot imagine going through this back-to-back intense *"bumpiness."*

There is a point that I want to drive home, and it is important to consider the timeline of events. I looked at the timelines in my study Bible regarding the book of Acts and when Paul was arrested. I then compared it to when some of Paul's epistles were written. I was excited by what I found.

It gives the contextual information for Acts. It states that Paul was imprisoned around A.D. 60-62. I enjoy the book of Philippians so much that I was curious to see when it was written in relation to this imprisonment. The timeline showed that Philippians was written in AD. 60-62 when Paul was imprisoned in Rome.[6]

For example, when Paul wrote about **contentment** in Philippians 4, he was right in the middle of intense life events. He wrote Philippians in the middle of huge bumps!

I am humbled by Paul and his right responses. He lived through consecutive life-threatening situations, but he was willing to learn contentment through them. He trusted God, despite these horrific experiences. He genuinely learned to say "*Okay, God.*" How awesome!

The Best Example—Jesus

Here is where we find the best example of "*Okay, God.*" Let us consider Jesus's time in the Garden of Gethsemane and His heartfelt prayer to His Heavenly Father.

Elizabeth George writes the following about the point in Jesus's life when He was getting close to sacrificing His life for sinful humanity.

It was the challenge He faced during His final days. His time had finally come—and what was ahead? Betrayal by His disciples. Misunderstanding from His family and followers. Rejection from mankind. Hostility and persecution. An angry mob, angry leaders, and angry people. Verbal and physical assault. An unjust sentence. The excruciating pain of crucifixion. Death. And, worst of all, momentary separation from His heavenly Father. From the human perspective, Jesus was losing all He had: His life, His family, His ministry, His friends, and His personal dignity.

Yet, His heavenly Father had commanded that He die for these sinners, and Jesus obeyed. Doing so would benefit others—including you and me!—because His death would be for sinners like us. So, acting in love, Jesus gave Himself as a sacrifice, a ransom for others (Matt. 20:28).7

These above thoughts were surely going through Jesus's mind when He went to the Garden of Gethsemane to pray. Let us consider Matthew 26. We see the plot to kill Jesus, and we see that Judas agreed to betray Jesus. Going into the Garden, Jesus was aware that he would soon be betrayed (Matt. 26:23). When we examine more of chapter 26, we cannot imagine Jesus's emotional stress. He was sorrowful, as He fell on His face to pray. On a physical level, He did not desire to die, yet He wanted to do God's will most of all. It must have been emotionally difficult to face (Matt. 26:38-39).

Jesus is our supreme example. While in the Garden, He went to His Heavenly Father in *three* major prayer sessions (Matt. 26:39, 42, 44). He begged God the Father to let this *cup* pass (His upcoming lot of crucifixion). Yet, in each of His prayer sessions, Jesus was sure to include that He knew it was the will of God the Father that He must follow.

In these verses, we see that it is not sinful to be in agony and to pray for some painful thing to be removed. Yet, like Jesus, we must include praying for the strength to *submit* to the *answer* that God gives.

Elizabeth George goes on to write about the results of the Garden's prayer sessions: "Nothing about Jesus' circumstances changed! After agonizing in prayer, He was *still* going to go to the cross, *still* going to be crucified, *still* going to die, but He went to the cross sustained by God's love, joy, and peace."[8] Jesus left the Garden that night with the strength to say *"Okay, God"* to His Heavenly Father.

Chapter's Concluding Thoughts

When my daughter was much younger, she ran up to me one afternoon asking if we had "crust." *Hmmmm, I thought, what in the world does she mean?* I asked her to repeat what she needed, and she said, "Do we have 'crust' for our teeth? The commercial said it's the best at cleaning teeth!" *Oooooh, I get it,* I thought, as I had to respond without giggling. I proclaimed, "Yes, we do have some of that!" She was quite satisfied. She assumed that if the commercial said it, it must be true.

We know the Bible to be true (and profitable—2 Tim. 3:16-17). Life would be easier if we would just practice what we believe. Adherence to the Bible truths and having faith in God through our bumps will help keep our lives joy-filled and spiritually on the right track. May we genuinely *learn*, through life's bumps, to honestly say *"Okay, God"* instead of *"Woah, God."*

Application Thoughts for Chapter 6

1. In what way(s) are you guilty of saying *"Woah, God?"* (You may not even be purposely trying to have a negative response.) Try to think through if there are any ways you could be saying *"Okay, God"* instead.

2. You may have meditated on Job 38-41 in chapter 3's application questions, but please consider these chapters in Job one more time. Do you have a particular trial, in which considering God's line of questions can encourage you to have a better perspective?

3. Is there an opportunity to practice or *learn* contentment in a specific area of your life? I encourage you to read through Philippians 4 and write down any Biblical truths that encourage you to have a more God-honoring response in a particular hardship.

4. When necessary, I urge you to pray that God will give you the strength to say, "not my will, but Your will be done!" Where do you need to surrender to God's will?

MATTERS OF THE HEART

Core Principle 4: Our heart can cause problems!

I ENJOY READING FOX NEWS articles by Joshua Rogers. He is a Christian writer who writes clever opinion pieces for FOX NEWS that deal with *life-lived*. Here is an excerpt from his article, *Thank God for that Awful Lady in the Lexus*.

The other day, I was just minding my own business, trying to get to work, when a woman in a black Lexus brought out the worst in me.

I was trying to park in a garage in downtown Washington, D.C., which is a challenge. I have little time to get to the garage after dropping off my daughter at school, and if I'm a minute late, the price goes up from $14 to $21. Time is of the essence.

Once you get to the garage, it doesn't matter which side of the street you're on, you have to wait your turn to get in. Everybody understands that — everybody but the lady in the black Lexus, apparently.

I was patiently waiting my turn when she drove up, ignored everyone in line, and zipped right up to Tony, the friendly security guard, who checked her ID and let her go. That surprised me because he normally doesn't allow cutting in line.

When I drove up, Tony looked at me with a defeated expression and said, "Bro, she's been doing that for years. There's no use in trying to stop her. She won't listen."

Her sense of entitlement made me angry, and as I pulled up behind her, I imagined how great it would feel to ram into the back of her car. There's no way I would do that, but something more tempting was the thought of seeing her in the garage and saying something like, "You know, I can't imagine what a nightmare it would be to be married to you." Ouch.

As I parked my car, the Holy Spirit pricked my conscience and showed me something: By reacting to the woman in the Lexus, I had actually become like her — maybe even worse...

People like that woman are actually a blessing to me. Their ability to provoke me to imagine things like ramming into the back of her car or telling her off is like an X-ray into my soul. It's opportunity for the Holy Spirit to say, "Hey, in case you haven't noticed, you've got issues with pride, resentment, and unforgiveness. I've allowed this person in your life to bring those things out so you'll realize how badly you still need to learn from Me every day."

Let's rejoice when we get unpleasantly blessed by people like the lady in the black Lexus. They've been sent to reveal, for better or worse, what's really going on inside of us. And regardless of whether those people ever change, Jesus can use them to bring changes in us that might never have happened otherwise.[1]

What a neat perspective. People and the bumps they can create for us are windows to our hearts! How we respond to trials shows us what is going on inside of us.

So, what does our heart drive us to do? When life gets *bumpy*, do we get fearful, angry, irritable, obnoxious, withdrawn, or something else—?

Right Use of Our Hearts

In the Gospels, we see Jesus's teachings about the heart. In Matthew 22:34-39, the Pharisees were gathered, and a lawyer asked Jesus to state the most important commandment in the Law. Jesus's response explained what our hearts should be doing in relationship with God. We should be loving God with all our HEARTS.

Let us briefly look at the word *heart* in the original Greek. It refers to: "the seat of the inner self" and is used figuratively in the New Testament as the "seat of desires, feelings, affections, passions, and impulses."[2]

We ought to be loving God with all our inner self, affections, and desires. This is the greatest commandment. To love God correctly looks like obedient trust and resultant praise, *even* on a bumpy road.

Heart of the Matter—Proverbs 4:20-27

The heart of the matter is the matter of the *heart!* Our heart can get us into trouble. If we desire relief from our trials more than we desire God's spiritual plan of growth for us, we will become *disheartened* and unable to please Him.

Kelly was to-the-point when she wrote about the physical *core*:

The core is the center—the internal glue that holds everything else together...These muscles are designed to stabilize your entire body. They are designed to help support and protect your vital organs. These core muscles are designed to support and stabilize. —[3]

What we will see below, in Proverbs 4, will shine a light on the similar importance that our *spiritual hearts* will have on our spiritual *core*. The heart is that important. It acts like the "glue" that holds us together. We will focus the rest of this chapter and the next on this matter of the heart.

I invite you to read Proverbs 4:20-27.

Wiersbe writes that, "As God's children, we need His loving counsel, and He gives it to us in this book (Proverbs)."[4] It is safe to say that Proverbs has wisdom-filled instruction that can be applied into the life of any child of God.

There are two things to consider about our passage.

- Prov. 4:20-22: Our heart is *receiving*.

  o Our <u>ears</u> should be accepting and heeding wisdom.

  o Our <u>eyes</u> should be holding on to wisdom that we receive.

- Prov. 4:23-27: Our heart is doing the *acting*. It is responding to what has been received.

Heart

The following is a *heavy-hitting* verse in our passage. We will look at it in different chunks.

Keep your heart with all diligence, for out of it spring the issues of life (Prov. 4:23).

The Old Testament's use of *heart* is similar to the New Testament's use. It regards the "inner person, self, the seat of thought and emotion..."[5] Unger writes that, "The heart is the innermost center of the natural condition of man...the heart is also the center of the feelings and affections of joy, of pain..."[6]

Our passions and resultant choices in life stem from what is taking place at the heart level.

Biblical Counselor, Tim Keeter, has a helpful chart.[7]

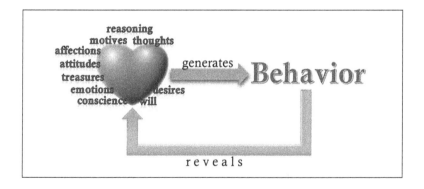

What is it in life that we are desiring, treasuring, or reasoning as so important that we *must* have it? Where are our innermost affections? Let us consider a few examples of what someone may be treasure.

- Freedom from chronic pain

- A nicer boss...or a pay raise

- Healing from sickness

- A car that starts every time

- A family free from fighting

None of these, in and of themselves, are evil. However, what is our attitude when we cannot have our most highly treasured desires? If we are not careful, we will begin to have a heart that demands relief. We will focus on our desires and lose sight of God's sovereignty and purpose for trials. As a result, we will lack faith. We will be failing at the previous three *core* principles listed in this book.

Keeter's chart shows that what we desire moves into behavior. If we are not careful, our desire for a better boss, for example, could lead us to start purposely arriving to work late. Or maybe it could drive us to gossip about him to our coworkers. Ironically, our behavior leads us to see what was in our heart in the first place. It is a big cycle.

Keep/Guard

Keeping or *guarding* of the heart comes in to play (Prov. 4:21, 23). The Hebrew words for *keep* in these verses are different, though they are synonymous. *Samar* (Prov. 4:21) means to "watch, observe, guard, be careful, be secured."[8] *Nasar* (Prov. 4:23) means to "guard, watch, protect, keep, preserve."[9] *The Complete Word Study Bible* adds that this term for *keep* "refers to people's maintaining things entrusted to them, especially to keeping the truths of God in both actions and mind...our hearts, in turn, ought to be maintained in a right state."[10]

Our heart must be guarded. Why should we guard are hearts? What is the big deal?

Issues of Life

The second half of Proverbs 4:23 lays it on the line for us: *for out of it spring the issues of life.* The *it* refers to the heart that is to be so well guarded. Your heart determines the course of your life. Everything you do flows from it, so it is important to watch over it.

Bruce Waltke, in his commentary, *The Book of Proverbs*, does not beat around the bush. He writes that the heart "must be reckoned as more important than anything else that needs to be restrained."[11] He goes on to write about the specifics regarding the end of 4:23. Regarding the phrase *for out of it,* he emphasizes that it is the heart that governs all activity."[12]

Waltke explains, "Since the heart is the center of all of a person's emotional-intellectual-religious-moral activity, it must be safeguarded above all things."[13]

The *core* of our decisions in life stem from what is taking place in our hearts. The heart is the source of all our actions and behavior. The heart is driving what we do. Scary!

Active. This is what our heart is...ACTIVE! We must guard it, guard it above all.

The Important Miscellaneous

We are not going to delve into much detail about the remaining verses in our section (Prov. 4:24-27), but let us briefly consider them. These following verses deal with the *actions* of the heart.

As a result of appropriate guarding of the heart, we ought to be mindful to guard the following:

- What our mouth speaks (Prov. 4:24)

- What our eyes look at (Prov. 4:25)

- Where our feet take us (Prov. 4:26-27)

A Frog Dissection...Its Heart!

Certain aspects of the *physical* heart can apply to this chapter. I never thought about the following concept until my young children were recently blessed with the opportunity to do a frog dissection at a Christian STEM-based resource center for homeschooling families. It is called Glen's Gizmos, owned by Joel and Roxanna Thomas.[14]

During the dissection, Joel Thomas, spoke about the frog's heart and how it was enveloped in a fluid sac. Joel talked about some of the purposes of this. One purpose was to protect the frog's other organs from the beating strength of the heart.[15]

I was very intrigued by this concept. Due to its strength, I had never considered the need of the physical heart to be restrained. After the dissection, I went home and did further study. I wanted to read about the human heart since I had just studied the heart of a frog with my children.

Here is what I learned about the physical human heart from a practical website. The author, Matt Quinn, deals with the heart's *pericardium*. He writes, "In scientific terms, the pericardium is a **fibro-serous**, fluid-filled sack that surrounds the muscular body of the heart and the roots of the great vessels..."[16]

Quinn compares this heart concept to an orange. He states, "If the heart is the fun, interesting inside bit of an orange, the **pericardium** could be compared to the peel around it."[17]

There is no way I could effectively paraphrase the purposes of the pericardium! I looked at many reliable websites that stated similar information. I really liked Quinn's verbiage on the topic; therefore, I will pull a large quote from his article:

The pericardium has many physiological roles, the most important of which are detailed below:

- *Fixes the heart in the mediastinum and limits its motion. Fixation of the heart is possible because the pericardium is attached to the diaphragm, the sternum, and the tunica adventitia (outer layer) of the great vessels.*

- *Prevents overfilling of the heart. The relatively inextensible fibrous layer of the pericardium prevents the heart from increasing in size too rapidly, thus placing a physical limit on the potential size of the organ.*

- **Lubrication.** *A thin film of fluid between the two layers of the serous pericardium reduces the friction generated by the heart as it moves within the thoracic cavity.*

- **Protection from infection.** *The fibrous pericardium serves as a physical barrier between the muscular body of the heart and adjacent organs prone to infection, such as the lungs.*[18]

I will not even pretend to understand what those medical terms mean! I like the first pericardium role listed, though. It fixes the heart in its place and limits its motion. This sounds exactly like what Joel Thomas taught about a frog's heart. If not for the fluid-filled sac, the heart could become too extreme.

This sounds like the spiritual heart! If not kept *in check*, who knows what kind of trouble it could cause!

This why the guarding is necessary. I picture the pericardium and its layers to be like the Holy Spirit and the Word of God. To keep us on the right track, we must guard our heart and be led by the truth of Scripture. The Holy Spirit can use the Word of God in our lives to keep us on the right path.

Chapter's Concluding Thoughts

We looked at practical verses to keep in mind when we choose to guard our hearts. When we guard our hearts well, we will be on track to please God. Elizabeth George puts it well: "A heart responsive to

God and His ways leads to a life of obedience—and these proven guidelines can help us stay on God's path."[19]

On the other hand, though, if we do not maintain a heart of trust, we will falter at the smallest of bumps. Even worse, all we can hope for is a *good luck* during a big trial. It is much easier to be obedient in our responses when we guard appropriately.

Application Thoughts for Chapter 7

1. In what main area of your heart have you found yourself not guarding enough?

2. What are some possible consequences for not guarding your heart enough and then falling into a specific sinful trap?

3. What Bible verse(s) can you meditate on and delight in to fill your heart with truth?

4. What specific and creative things can you do or put in place to help curb any possible lapses of your heart?

The Heart Continued...

PRETEND THAT YOU and I are in the same room and that I am holding a disposable water bottle filled with *water*. I then use my hand to bump the water bottle. What came out? (Water...) Why?

It was not simply the bump that made the water come out. The water came out because there was *water* inside. If there had been lemonade inside, lemonade would have come out; therefore, it is not really the bump that can be blamed for the water coming out. Hmmm....

What is the point? The <u>result</u> of the <u>same</u> type of bump to a water bottle filled with water will look completely different than a water bottle filled with lemonade or car oil. Kevin Carson taught this illustration.[1]

Let us consider the *bump* as a life circumstance or trial of some kind. If we are *bumped* in life with someone being snippy with us, what will come out? Will a heart of anger come out...bitterness...or a desire for peace and unity? I believe it all depends on how much we have guarded our hearts.

If we are bumped with traffic at the most inopportune time, what will come out? Will a heart of impatience come out...a lack of trust in God's goodness and sovereignty...or thanksgiving? It depends on how well we have guarded our hearts.

If we are bumped with a scary health diagnosis, what will come out? In a big trial, this is where we see our heart at its best (or worst). Again, our response depends on how we have guarded our hearts.

It is not easy!

In Proverbs 4, we saw how important it is to guard our hearts. If we are not careful to guard, then ungodly responses to trials will result. How do we *know* when we are on the *wrong track*, though? In any given trial, we may not be purposefully responding in a hostile way towards God's plan, but we could respond poorly all the same. How do we know if our heart is *out of whack* regarding a trial?

Idea of Idols of the Heart

Many solid books have been written on this topic alone. I will use material from a book that I highly recommend, *Idols of the Heart* by Elyse Fitzpatrick. She devotes her time to share what the heart can be guilty of and then how our affections can be steered the right way instead.

How do we know if our heart has been misled and that we are pleasing ourselves instead of pleasing God? Elyse explains it well. "If you're willing to sin to obtain your goal or if you sin when you don't get what you want, then your desire has taken God's place and you're functioning as an idolater."[2]

She also writes, "What must I have for life to be meaningful or happy? If I answer that question with anything other than God Himself, then that's what functions as a god for me...Idols aren't just stone statues. No, idols are the thoughts, desires, longings, and expectations that we worship in the place of the true God."[3]

Sally's example:

Sally *desires* to have a beautiful garden full of lush vegetables and fruit. There is no sinful act in this desire. Oh, but watch out... Sally desires it more and thinks about it more and more. She starts looking at gardening magazines in the MIDDLE OF CHURCH! She is starting to be drawn away by this desire. Then, she finds the perfect garden picture of beans growing in her garden. But wait, she does not have any beans to plant, and she has already reached her budget. Plus, she cannot go out and buy the expensive grow lamp, much less the stand that comes with it. These are the ideas that the magazine showed. That desire, though, has become too great, and her heart is ensnared. As a result, she goes to her neighbor's garage when he is in the backyard mowing and steals his grow lamps.[4]

How sad. A perfectly sinless desire became something her heart wrapped itself around. She flat-out sinned versus having a heart that desired to love and honor God above even her desire for a great garden. She did not follow the greatest command to love God above all. Her heart got in the way. Do we see how quickly things can go downhill if we listen to our heart over what God wants for our life?

Sally had an idol of her heart by _sinning to get what she wanted_.

That was a rather extreme example, but at the heart level, aren't we all guilty? If we are not careful, we may scowl (at least internally) at the family who could afford a two-week vacation to Hawaii, while we are stuck in an extreme-weather climate to our disliking.

This example, about the Hawaiian vacation, shows an idol of the heart that can be exhibited due to us *not getting what we want. Thou shalt not covet, right?*

Perhaps we may impatiently and unkindly whisk our kids out the door because we too strongly desire to get the perfect parking spot at the big sale! All these scenarios picture our heart in the same light as in Sally's scenario. An unguarded heart desiring something too greatly can cause us to sin against people *and* a holy God who desires our heart's love more than any earthly desire.

Small bumps are indeed irritating. If we are struggling to honor God in the small situations, we may very well struggle in the big. We should strive to practice guarding our heart and choose to keep our focus on God's bigger plan.

Cupping of the Hand Example

Dave Perry (who performed my wedding ceremony) walked through the following illustration in a sermon. He held up both hands, palms side up, with the pinkies touching. This made a bowl shape. He explained that if what we are desiring can rest in that bowl (figuratively), and if our hands are still able to be open, then we can rest assured that our desire is not idolatrous. If, however, we figurately wrap our hands around that same desire and we are "fighting" to keep our hands wrapped around it, then we are probably making that desire idolatrous.[5]

The point that Dave was making is that we must be willing to let God do what He wants with our desires. Are we grasping on to our desires with such a tight grip that we are not willing to have any other outcome than *our way*? Or are we letting the desires rest in our hands and remain openly raised up toward heaven?

Remember that Job praised God when he lost all that was valuable. We, too, must not wrap our hands around desires. If we too tightly enclose our hands around what we want, we may find ourselves sinning to get the desired thing *or* sinning in our responses for not getting the desired thing.

A Brief Look at Psalm 119:11

"Your word I have hidden in my heart, that I might not sin against You" (Ps. 119:11).

The best way to guard the heart is to fill it with God's Word. When we delight in God's Word and fill our hearts with it, we guard our hearts.

Here is a quote from Pastor Dean Clarkson. He said this about using Psalm 119:11 in our lives: "The secret weapon (God's Word) put in a secret place (our heart) stops future sin."[6]

The Pure in Heart

Our church's Sunday School class went through Jesus's Sermon on the Mount. We utilized a book by D. Martyn Lloyd-Jones called, *Studies in the Sermon on the Mount*. In this sermon, Jesus spoke on many important qualities. One of them is, "Blessed are the pure in heart..." (Matt. 5:8). Lloyd-Jones writes: "Who are the pure in heart? Essentially, as I am going to show you, they are those who are mourning about the impurity of their hearts."[7]

He also writes, "This pureness of heart, therefore, corresponds to 'singleness'. It means, if you like, 'without folds'; it is open, nothing hidden."[8]

I really like the word picture of *without folds* and *nothing hidden*. My children enjoy pre-treating their stained clothes. (They love spraying the stains.) On the really dirty parts of the clothes, though, I typically go back through and make sure there were no hidden stains that were missed because of the creases on the clothes. There have been many times that I had to spray what was otherwise hidden.

This is very much the case with our hearts. If we do not carefully purge the bad—and hidden—parts in our hearts, then roots will hang on and imbed stronger and deeper inside.

King David saw the need to pray for a clean heart and for a renewed spirit (Ps. 51:10).

We will mess up. The key is to see progress in our Christian maturity.

Chapter's Concluding Thoughts

When we learn to trust and accept God's plan, spiritual growth will take place. However, we need to be on-guard because spiritual growth does not stay on a guaranteed trajectory. We can sometimes spiritually flounder, especially if we do not respond well through a particular trial. We must *proactively* guard our hearts since they are so *reactive*.

Application Thoughts for Chapter 8

1. What do you desire or treasure most in life? (Think back to Keeter's chart).

2. Has it become a sinful desire or not? How can you tell? (Have you sinned or wanted to sin to have your desire fulfilled? Have you sinned because you did not get what is treasured?)

3. If you are struggling in this area, I encourage you to write out and meditate on specific Bible verses to help keep you on the right track. If necessary, bring in a trusted friend to get *on board* with you to help encourage you with the Word of God.

4. Are there hidden sinful creases or folds in your heart that you need to confess?

Keep On Keeping On!

Core **Principle 5: Perseverance is necessary in our journey.**

SUPERHEROES CAN BE fun for all ages. Kids zooming around the house with a cape, grown-ups spending money (and lost sleep) on movie tickets. We know superheroes are made up, but they are still fun!

Take *Superflex*, a superhero with a goal to defeat *Social Unthinkables*. (This superhero is part of a curriculum designed to teach young children how to improve in their social skills).[1] I was introduced to it by Chelsea Hill and Trina Volk from Prism Pediatric Therapy.[2]

The curriculum has a fun plot line. It has a big superhero set-up and includes storylines and characters in a town called *Social Town*. The superhero's name is *SuperFlex*, and his job is to defeat the *Unthinkables* (the social problems) that enter *Social Town*. Some of the *Unthinkables* are called:

- RockBrain

- Glassman

- DOF (Destroyer of Fun)

- Mean Gene[3]

SuperFlex then gets to use his flexible problem-solving strategies to defeat these *Unthinkables*.

Though it is not a Bible-based curriculum, I do like how it showed practical picture examples and scenarios of some of the wrong behaviors that children exhibit. In our homeschool 'circle time' one year, I used targeted Bible verses to go with the concepts so that my children would see what the Bible teaches about the behaviors addressed in the curriculum. Plus, it was good for my children to strategize ways to make God-honoring choices.

Spiritual Unthinkables

One day, I thought about how Christian adults can also be guilty of having *spiritual unthinkables* enter our *Spiritual Town*.

Here are a few *spiritual unthinkables* that I made up to help make a point:

- Faith Lacker

- Lack 'O Joy

- Lazy Pants

- Tight Waddy

- Discontent Grumpster

- Perseverer Antitheses

We must strategize how to defeat these *spiritual unthinkables*, too! Here is the catch, though, we cannot do this on our own! We need divine strength like we discussed in previous chapters.

In previous chapters we were challenged to watch our responses to trials. We need a lot less *"Woah, God"* in our lives (at least I do). Yet, life is still hard. The bumps either remain, or new ones pop up. How do we keep living without quitting? Perseverance! Easier said than done, of course, but it should be our goal since we have God's resources at our disposal.

We also considered the great example of Jesus. God the Father gave Him strength. We have this same strength from which we can draw. We can be encouraged by the following Bible passages, as we take them to heart.

Psalm 28

This Psalm, written by King David, involves wicked and deceptive people. David cried out to God and asked God not to take him away with the wicked. It may sound like David wished evil on them in some sort of revengeful way. Wiersbe writes in his Old Testament commentary that, "David's prayer was not an expression of personal revenge but a call for God to fulfill His covenant and bring righteousness and peace into the land."[4] Either way, being around the wicked who were out to do him harm, is not a particularly wonderful set of circumstances in David's life.

Here is why David could keep a good perspective, despite dealing, once again, with wicked people: he prayed about it. He did not go ho-hum-life stinks; he prayed. He prayed a lot. His prayers kept his focus on the right area: on God and not his personal circumstances! In verse 7, we see that *faith* made the change in David's heart.

This Psalm shows us that David's life was continually filled with wicked men out to get him, but the following verse is very telling for David's right perspective:

"The Lord is my strength and shield; My heart trusted in Him, and I am helped; Therefore my heart greatly rejoices, and with my song I will praise Him" (Ps. 28:7).

What did David state so well in this verse?

1. God was his strength and shield (think of protection).

2. God could be trusted whole-heartedly.

3. David's heart could then praise and rejoice.

Trust brings praise. (What can be said of the opposite?) Our praise keeps our focus on God no matter what transpires in our lives. If we do not apply what David did in verse 7, we may very well become bitter along life's bumpy roads.

Psalm 46

The first few verses in this Psalm are practical for dealing with fears. Consider these two main points:

1. God is the One who gives strength.

2. God is always present in our lives.

When my daughter was around 4 years old, our city had a small snow event one morning. The meteorologist had said the night before that it would pass quickly. Sometime in the morning hours, the snow would turn to rain and melt any accumulation. So, when I saw the snow that next morning, I decided to go quickly downstairs (before the kids woke up) and dig out their snow gear from our bin. By the time I got upstairs, my daughter had already awoken and was scared that I was seemingly not around. She had been calling, and I had not come. I am sure there were tears in her eyes. I remember reassuring her that I would never leave her alone. In my mind, at least, I knew the kids were safe.

Here is why I like Psalm 46. It reiterates that God is with us, and He gives strength even if we do not realize it to its full potential all the time. He is not going to leave us in our despair, *in our tears.*

During instability, on a variety of levels, it is so easy to despair and lose faith.

Personal Example

Perhaps you can take a moment to think about the most recent time you were tempted to despair. For me, it was when my son was a baby. He was my second born, but even before his birth, there were some concerns for his health during my pregnancy. The midwives and doctors disagreed if he was just 'small for gestational age' or if he had true growth restriction. Time and time again, I had ultrasounds checking growth, and I had checkups watching for his movement. I was admitted to the hospital to have him induced at 37 weeks. He was born shortly after. Not surprisingly, the doctors monitored his blood sugar levels, but he was otherwise healthy. It turned out that he was *just* 'small for gestational age' and did not have growth restrictions, which was a blessing. He was a healthy baby boy.

When he was one month old, he started constantly moaning, in immense pain, and then caught a fever. I called the nurse helpline in the middle of the night, and the nurse said to rush him (as safely as possible) to the emergency room. At the time, and for many days to come, they did not know the specific cause of the problem. So, the health team gave him many sets of antibiotics, just for proactive measures. (Little did I know, at the time, that my life would quickly turn to times of great despair because of his time in the hospital.) After many days of my son being pumped with antibiotics, test results came in, and the medical team ruled out several options. They were able to take him off the antibiotics.

Please know that I am not anti-medical care, nor am I against the use of antibiotics, but I did not know what these antibiotics did to my son's five-pound body for many months to come. All I knew from his return home from the hospital from that point, to what felt like an eternity forward, was that he was more than just your 'average not-so-great baby sleeper'. He woke me, what felt like constantly, and not because he was hungry. I would call his pediatrician's office in tears, but they offered less-than-helpful advice. Fast forward many months. There was no way that a then seven-month-old, should be having such terrible times with eating and sleeping.

I remember being by my son's crib one night, beyond the point of exhaustion, wondering if God really knew what I could handle. Of course, I *knew* that *He knew*, yet in my despair, I sure did start to doubt that I could continue to handle such limited and broken-up sleep. I did struggle to *trust*. It took a lot of singing of Bible verses, *over and over and over and over*, in my mind. Verses, put to song, like *Rejoice in the Lord*, and *This is the Day that the Lord Has Made*, were my mind's rallying cry to get me through those dark nights. I really believe that these verses kept me sane. Praise God, He knew when to halt this pain (for our son and for us). Our chiropractor recommended a Naturopathic Doctor. God used her as an instrument to help heal my son's body of the after-effects of the antibiotics.

Looking back at Psalm 46, the first verse is packed with goodness and proclaims that *God is our refuge and strength*. Refuge has to do with a place of safety and protection, like a shelter on a rainy day. This verse does not say that God is our refuge to make the trouble go away. No, it means that God is our refuge *in* the trouble.

God is also our strength. Our power in life to get through hardships comes from God. It does not say to pull from our own strength because this would not cut it. The end of verse 1 reads that this help is *very present*. God is very available, always providing help, in order to provide us a place of refuge and strength in our extreme discomfort. That is encouraging!

The next verse proclaims, "Therefore, we will not fear..." In unstable times, God is at work and is there for us. Let us look at verse 10 to end this section.

"Be still and know that I am God...!" (Ps. 46:10a).

I have notes written in my Bible from 15 years ago about this verse. Similar thoughts are in Wiersbe's commentary: Be still; take your hands off; relax. Allow God to be God and do not try to micromanage your life![5]

We must rely on our strength from God, or we would too easily give up and throw in the towel!

Let us look at just one New Testament example:

Hebrews 12:1-2

"Therefore we also, since we are surrounded by so great a cloud of witnesses, let us lay aside every weight, and the sin which so easily ensnares us, and let us run with endurance the race that is set before us, looking unto Jesus, the author and finisher of our faith, who for the joy that was set before Him endured the cross, despising the shame, and has sat down at the right hand of the throne of God (Heb. 12:1-2).

Here is an important preface before we look more at Hebrews 12. It is important to note to whom this *great cloud of* witnesses is referring at the beginning of this chapter. Immediately preceding Hebrews 12 is what some call the *Wall of Faith.* Hebrews 11 lists multiple individuals who trusted God through difficult times. Many commentaries speak to these *witnesses* as those referred to in Hebrews 11. Wiersbe writes that, "These people are not witnessing what we are doing; rather, they are bearing witness to us that God can see us through."[6] These *witnesses* from chapter 11 make great examples for us to exhibit faith in hard times.

Old Testament Joseph

My favorite on the Hebrews 11 *Wall of Faith* list is Joseph. We see details of his life in Genesis 37-50. Here are some highlights of Joseph's life and how he went through difficult times.

His brothers hated Joseph. They were jealous of him and conspired to kill him. At least his brother, Reuben, talked them out of that and threw him in a pit instead. Then, they sold him to Ishmaelite traders who brought him to Egypt, and the brothers lied to their dad about what happened to Joseph.

Joseph was in a new land, with no hope of his father looking for him. He was a slave for Potiphar, a captain of the guard under Pharaoh. God was with Joseph, though (Gen. 39:2), and he became successful in his new role. Yet, Potiphar's wife told lies about Joseph, which caused Joseph to be thrown into prison. Joseph was eventually released from prison to help Pharaoh figure out his dreams, yet this was after years of being unjustly in prison!

Joseph was brought into leadership after helping Pharaoh, and God used Joseph to protect His people during famine. Joseph's life was certainly filled with hardship, though he never gave up doing what was right and serving others.

At the end of Genesis, his brothers were in Joseph's presence and humbly offered to be Joseph's servants (Gen. 50:18). I love Joseph's response. With all the evil done to him, he told his brothers not to fear. Though they had done much evil to Joseph, God used it all for good (Gen. 50:19-21). Joseph did not blame God for his problems in life. Instead, he recognized God's over-arching plan. He kept a godly perspective. I view Joseph as a great example of resilience. He trusted God and persevered. It is no surprise that he made it to this *Wall of Faith* that comes just before our Hebrews 12 passage.

The beginning of Hebrews 12 is all about persevering in life's ups and downs. It is important to catch the phrase at the end of verse 1, "Let us run with endurance the **race that is set before us**" (emphasis added). We do not have full control over what happens in life. This is LIFE LIVED. This is where the "rubber meets the road." God has set a race *before us*, and we are to be prepared to endure.

Thankfully, the passage does not end there. The following verse tells us on whom our focus should be—Jesus! He endured a lot; we covered this previously. He is our supreme example for dealing with hardship. He endured, too. We are to *consider Him* so that we do not become weary and discouraged (Heb. 12:3).

To stay on track spiritually, we must have 20/20 focus on the right source. Our Hebrews 12 passage states that we need to look *unto Jesus* and *consider Him* in our life's hardships.

Analyzing a Helicopter Crash:

I remember being saddened when I saw the news push alert on my phone that Kobe Bryant had died in a helicopter crash. My brother, James, and I had watched his rookie season in the NBA. I felt saddened for Kobe's family due to his sudden death.

I read several articles about his helicopter crash. I preface this to say I do not mean any judgement toward the pilot or any of the choice-makers that day. It is a sad story, yet I learned much from one article that helped explain some tough concepts surrounding the crash.

It was through the Oregonian news organization that I read many informative articles about the crash. One particular article was entitled: *Kobe Bryant Helicopter Tried to Climb To Avoid Clouds Before Crash.*[7] In the article, different helicopter pilots were interviewed about the difficulties of flying in adverse weather, such as was the case in the Bryant crash.

Helicopter pilots place great importance on the machine's instruments. In this article, flight instructor, Randy Waldman, was interviewed and said, "A disoriented pilot might have only moments to avoid a fatal dive. If you're flying visually, if you get caught in a situation where you can't see out the windshield, the life expectancy of the pilot and the aircraft is maybe 10, 15 seconds, and it happens all the time, and it's really a shame."[8]

Another flight instructor, Jerry Kidrick, talked about how the pilot may have been disoriented because of his fast descent. "When that happens, he said, pilots must instantly switch from visual cues to flying the aircraft using only the machine's instruments...oftentimes, your body is telling you something different than what the instruments are telling you."[9] These pilot interviews broke my heart to read. Nobody wants to go through that fear.

We can apply these quotes to our spiritual lives. We cannot trust our fleshly perspective in life's trials any more than a pilot stuck in thick fog can trust his personal *visual cue.* Just as a pilot must be led by his machine's instruments, in a spiritual sense, our main instrument is God and what we learn about Him from the Bible. Based on Hebrews 12, our specific *instrument* in this context is Jesus as our baseline for what is right. This concept allows us to survive our disorienting trials that come up and surprise us like thick fog.

Other Supporting Bible Verses

Here are a few other scriptures that deal with perseverance:

- 1 Peter 1:6-7—Trials are for a season, and they are precious in our growth if we keep the right perspective.

- Galatians 6:9—Press on!

- Colossians 1:9-11 Walk worthy and be strengthened by His mighty power.

- 2 Timothy 4:16-17 People forsook Paul and did him harm, but he stated that the Lord stood with him and strengthened him.

Chapter's Concluding Thoughts

To close this chapter on perseverance, I will leave you with one last thought. In 2 Timothy 2:1-3, Paul writes to Timothy to encourage him to be strong in Christ and to endure like a soldier. Spiritually speaking, we sometimes need back-up, just like soldiers do in war. Try and find encouraging friends that will help uplift you spiritually, and vice versa! We can come alongside and help lift one another up when we are desperate to defeat some spiritual *unthinkable*. There are times when we need each other to help strategize and pray.

In the last two chapters, we will consider specific strategies to help us in our endeavors to honor God through our bumps along life's road.

Application Thoughts for Chapter 9

1. What spiritual *unthinkable* may be weighing you down? What behaviors are being exhibited as a result?

2. Think again on Psalm 28 and what King David dwelled on in his hardship:

   - God was his strength and shield (think of protection).

   - God could be trusted whole-heartedly.

   - David's heart could then praise and rejoice.

Could any of these above points be gently massaged into your heart to help you persevere through a particular trial?

3. Are there areas in life where you may need to be still and take your hands off...and then trust?

4. If you struggle with perseverance, read through and dwell on the Bible Truths found in Psalm 28, Psalm 46, and Hebrews 12:1-3. Also, try to memorize some of the verses listed at the end of this chapter. They are:

   - 1 Peter 1:6-7

   - Galatians 6:9

   - Colossians 1:9-11

   - 2 Timothy 4:16-17

Section 3
The Application

Counseling Categories

Pretend that a special seven-year-old in your life has just come to you with a unique request. Maybe this is your child, a grandchild, niece or nephew, or the child for whom you nanny. The child asks you for help on a *dreaded school project*!

Ah, you are relieved, though, when you hear it is *just* following six simple steps for making snowflakes. Plus, helpful pictures are included. The steps are seemingly simple:

1. Fold the square paper in half to make a triangle.

2. Fold the paper in half again.

3. Fold the paper in thirds.

4. Cut off the excess at the bottom to make a straight edge.

5. Cut desired shapes in the folded triangle.

6. Open the paper to see your **circular** snowflake.[1]

Once you and your special child work through steps 1-3, you feel good about the speed and ease through which you have worked. Then, you see step 4, and you realize your tri-folded paper does not have any excess at the bottom to cut off. You decide to go with the flow, though. Afterall, you want to show your good 'flexibility' skills to your special child. You have your child continue to step 5 and then to step 6. Once the paper is unfolded, you realize that there is no circular snowflake. It is square, ugh! You both try again, *several times*. You decide this is not going well; you need another person to help.

If you look at the below picture, you will see that this is sadly a *true* story.

2

My sweet seven-year-old and I struggled with what others would consider a simple project (hence the left of the picture)! We had to wait until my husband came home. He, of course, figured it out right away. Even more exciting, we had a circular snowflake at the end (see the right side of the picture).

What is my point? Why do I have this silly example in this chapter (or even in this book)? Well, I had a craft-making *problem* (though not serious in the scheme of life, I know). Others would have not had this *problem,* but *I did.* Spiritually speaking, we are all at different levels. Plus, we sure can negatively vacillate depending on how much we have God's Word embedded in our hearts, ready to apply at moment's notice!

Spiritual setbacks can also frustrate us to no end. Think of what Paul wrote in Romans 7:18-25. He admits that nothing good comes from his fleshly desires. The thing he *wants* to do, he *does not,* and vice versa. He calls himself wretched.

It is no surprise then, that for some, there may be certain temptations (regarding responses) to life's bumps that are much more difficult to work though in a godly way, compared to another person. For instance, one person receiving a cancer diagnosis could be knocked off her feet so much that she turns from God. Yet, for another, a similar cancer diagnosis will drop her to her knees in prayer.

There will be times in life for each of us that we will have to *ask* for spiritual help, and that is OKAY. Like in that silly snowflake example, I am sure many people would not have needed help, but **I did**!

This is why I started this chapter with a silly example of a real need for help. When we are rocked in our world, we may very well have to take a step back and determine the category of help and guidance we may need to work through a particular circumstance.

I will break the rest of this chapter into three different *categories* to consider. Please understand that the categories I walk through are not representative of who has the weakest faith! My goal is for us to be able to "triage" where we may be in a particular spiritual struggle in life so that we know what type of help we may need.

Category 1: Initial Self-Counsel

Think of the race set before us in Hebrews 12 as the road of life. *Category One: Initial Self-Counsel* refers to general wear and tear on our spiritual bodies. This category, at its *core*, is vital even though someone does not yet need to seek outside help for proper godly responses to some trial. Nonetheless, there will be a bump at hand. The trial could be small or large. The size does not matter; it is how the heart responds to whatever the trial is.

Here is an example of what this could look like practically. Pretend you just had a last-minute flight cancelation. The airline over-booked. You were supposed to enjoy a quick weekend trip to sunny Florida. With this sudden cancelation (and finding out that there is not another flight out until *tomorrow)* you decide it is not worth it to re-book the flight. You are stewing about it all evening. Then, you get this conviction that God is not pleased with your sour attitude. You decide to study and meditate on Bible verses regarding what God thinks about complaining, and your heart is softened to be *okay with* God's plan.

This is considered self-counsel. It is using God's Word in your situation specifically to help you respond in a God-pleasing manner.

We should be in a consistent state of this initial self-counsel. Afterall, we often and actively struggle with specific sins.

One area that I was recently convicted of and chose to self-counsel regarded the weather. I realized that when people asked me how my week went, the response had something to do with my attitude toward the weather.

Here is an example conversation from last Fall:

Friend: How was your week?

Me: We loved it! We got to go outside and enjoy the sun! It was a wonderful week. (Translation: I loved, loved, loved standing out in the Fall sun. It was glorious! It made me so happy…)

The following week:

Friend: How was your week?

Me: Oh, the weather was so chilly! Because it rained a lot, we did not make it outside too much. It was a good-enough week, I guess.

At the end of Fall:

Friend: We should have an outdoor playdate sometime with the kids.

Me: That would be great! I am just so sad, though, how the weather is turning chillier. Hopefully we can find a day that is sunny.

I am certainly not inferring that it is bad to talk about the weather. It is just that I valued a good weather day *far* above a bad weather day. My contentment was based on the wrong thing.

So, for self-counsel, I had to make a plan. I had to dwell on passages like Ecclesiastes 7. God establishes a variety of days. I had to learn to accept what He brought regarding the weather. I then decided that I had to do something practical. I began to look out the living room window each morning and tell God, *"It's okay, God...whatever weather You bring, I accept!"* It seems silly enough, but it helped in my self-counsel.

Sometimes calling yourself out is enough. Just realizing a sin issue and bringing it to the forefront of the mind—and turning from the sin— may be sufficient to deal with the problem. Other times, it may take a more aggressive approach.

Category 2: Additional Self-Counsel/Accountability

What about those times in life that we aim to apply God's Word in certain situations, but we seem to keep failing? We must remember that we have been promised God's strength, but sometimes, we just seem to struggle to apply God's Word in the *heat* of our circumstance. Our failure is not a reflection of God not doing His part. It really is just a reflection of our fallen nature, and sometimes we struggle to apply God's Word in the middle of some circumstance.

Here is an example. You seem to continually harbor thoughts of discontentment in your job. This job may be staying home full time with your children. Maybe the job is full time in an office setting that is less than ideal for your liking, or the job may be one that causes much travel, and you are a homebody. Whatever the case, let us pretend you are discontented at work. You know it is sinful, and you pray about it, but you keep dwelling on your unhappiness.

You try some initial self-counsel. You make it your goal to read through Philippians 4:1-13 before work each day, but you seem to forget about applying it when your day turns lousy. Pretend on that weekend, your dear friend asks how work is going, and you admit to her that you hate it and are so unhappy. You tell her that you really need help to respond in a way that pleases God.

As a result of asking for help (because you rightfully admitted you needed it), you now have an accountability partner. In essence, this is someone who will walk beside you while you work through a spiritual problem and will encourage you to make godly choices. With help, spiritual victory can be found.

For the sake of our scenario, this accountability partner comes up with a practical idea for you to try. It is a simple, yet effective, idea for you to write out Philippians 4:11 on an index card and put it somewhere noticeable on your work desk. She also encourages you to put a few reminders in your phone that will pop up throughout your workday. It could be something like, "Are you pleasing God" or "Read Philippians 4:11." Your accountability partner then tells you that she will call you on Friday to see how the plan worked. This does not mean that the partner calls every Friday, though it could involve that. The goal, though, is that you have a plan in place that helps you gain spiritual victory.

Again, accountability may look quite different depending on the situation at hand, but if you need help, please ask someone you trust and who will uplift you spiritually.

I had a special accountability partner while I was dating (my now husband). Brittney Pauley was willing to ask me tough questions at any time. Years later, when we were not officially in an accountability relationship anymore, she was still the one I texted late one night when I was fearful about something related to a dangerous task my husband had to do while he was out of town. I trusted her, and she gave Biblical advice when I needed it.

Accountability groups can also be beneficial. Here is an interesting historical example of this category. Adoniram Judson, known as *America's first missionary*, spent his ministry days in Burma. According to the book, *Christian Heroes: Then & Now, Adoniram Judson, Bound for Burma*, Judson was approached in seminary to join a group of other men who were interested in mission work. Authors Janet and Geoff Benge wrote this about Judson being asked to join this group of men: "Their aim, Samuel Mills told him, was to help each other stay focused on missions, to pray for opportunities to go as missionaries..."[3]

Accountability can be more than just *reactive*. It can be *proactive*, too, to help each other stay on track with spiritual goals.

Category 3: Professional Counseling

Not every person will require this type of counseling in life. Yet, for some, there may be a need for a well-trained counselor to work through more difficult situations. I highly recommend the use of a Biblical Counselor. A Biblical Counselor will utilize the Bible as the driving force for life change.

I have trained under or worked specifically with counselors from the Association of Biblical Counseling. Regarding this group, its website mentions, "In short, we seek to bring biblical solutions for the problems people face, upholding that the method God has given to do this is truth in love."[4] I know there are many good Biblical Counseling clinics around the country that are not directly affiliated with an organization, yet they still use the Bible as the guide for life change. I recommend researching any counseling clinics in advance to see if they put the emphasis on the Bible as the means to affect life change.

There could be a myriad of reasons for someone needing to see a counselor. The type of problem is not the issue at hand. The important thing to note is it is OKAY to ask for help for an area of life that cannot be handled alone.

A solid Biblical counselor will ask appropriate probing questions to get to the heart of the matter. This counselor will then be able to see the *presenting problem*, and also discover *peripheral problems* along the way. A wise counselor will be able to utilize pinpointed Bible passages and give creative 'homework' to work through the presented issues. The end goal is for the counselee to have spiritual victory. Plus, the counselee can also leave with great Bible principles and tools to help with continued spiritual growth, even after the official counseling is done.

Personalized Application

With permission, I am writing about my friend, Heather Rivera. She is willing to let me share her story so that others may be encouraged. On her Facebook account (in February, 2021) she bravely posted about her struggles with depression. She wrote that she could not find a perfect quote about mental health. She stated, "Mental Health is hard in general, but what's even harder is admitting you are struggling with mental health."[5] She also mentioned how she felt defeated when she would become depressed, and then would pray, yet still not be okay. She then boldly stated, "But the truth is, it is okay to need help. When I admitted that, I was able to give myself grace and admit I needed help."[6]

Yes, it is indeed okay to get help from a counselor. It does not make you less of a Christian.

In the introduction, I mentioned how a Biblical Counselor helped me when I was experiencing specific driving anxieties resulting from a car accident. My chiropractor recommended I consider seeing a counselor based on what I shared with her about these anxieties.

I never 'planned' to have to receive help from a counselor, especially since all my graduate school electives were from the Biblical Counseling tract. I loved those classes, and I learned much about solid aspects about God's sovereignty, God's plan for Christian growth, a Christian's proper response, and the need to guard the heart. These were life-changing classes. I knew the *right stuff.*

However, I veered off course at some point after the car accident. I became fearful I would get in another crash. I have been in several accidents, yet this was the first with my children. Here is the part that got the best of me. I feared my children could not go through another one; so that meant I could not go through another one.

My counselor, Rosalie, learned of my *presenting problem*. I had anxieties of once again being bumped from behind, and I feared driving in big city traffic. Rosalie was wise, though, and through the questions I had to complete for her intake paperwork, she discovered the *peripheral*, too. I had become quite a "control freak" with the details that ran through my mind regarding the car accident. I would lose sleep from worry about accident details and the resultant health of one of my children. I was all over the place in my thoughts. I viewed this car accident as one huge inconvenience, and the adverse insurance company as the enemy.

Rosalie gently took me through specific passages about God's sovereignty and the purpose for trials. Some of the concepts she walked me through were similar to what I had learned in my counseling classes in school. She just specifically applied them to my case, and she offered me such an amazing reminder about particular Biblical principles that must affect all areas of life.

Through my counseling, Rosalie required me to do homework, though for me it was never a chore. She worked with me to come up with specific plans for when I was experiencing driving anxieties in traffic or if I was struggling with my worrisome thoughts in the middle of the night. It took work. I had to do my part in applying the truth of the Scriptures and work through our plans. God was so gracious to bring Rosalie alongside me. Seeing a counselor gave me tools to more effectively keep my eye turned toward Scripture.

A good Biblical counselor will be able to integrate ideal *homework* into one's practical life. Kelly once referenced the following about physical therapy *homework*.

Function and lifestyle integration were key to my clients' success. Understanding the world that every person lived in helped me be creative and realistic in what I had clients work through. I had to become very efficient and intentional about what I started to think of as 'real life rehabilitation'.[7]

Like with physical therapy, a Biblical counselor will be able to creatively give *intentional* homework that can be fleshed out practically in the clients' real world.

Chapter's Concluding Thoughts

I hope the above testimonies can bring encouragement or offer someone courage to take the step to see a counselor if it becomes necessary. Getting help, when needed, is a step towards victory. Praise God if someone can have spiritual victory without ever stepping foot in a counseling office. Yet, praise God for more specific professional help when it is needed.

Application Thoughts for Chapter 10

1. Is there an <u>active area</u> in your life where you could start to *self-counsel* against some sin? Write out verses that deal with this *active area*.

2. Be creative to deal with this *active area* head-on. I encourage you to write out a specific plan of attack.

3. Is there an area in life that you realize you may need an additional *player* to assist you in your spiritual walk? Do you have a plan on how to approach this person?

4. Do you see an opportunity to come alongside a friend and offer this friend some spiritual uplifting?

Concluding Strategies

To end the book, I wanted to leave you with some concluding strategies for applying Biblical principles in your life's bumps. These strategies can be utilized in the *self-counsel* or *additional self-counsel* categories that were discussed in the previous chapter. If nothing else, maybe this chapter can get your creative juices flowing to aid in your path to honor God. I think the key is to have a *plan* for when bumps arise and tempt you to despair. These strategies may look different for each person based on your circumstances and temptations. In whatever situation be creative and intentionally *do* your strategies.

Hopefully before these bumps arise, our spiritual *core* is already established (Think of the key principles listed throughout the book). Having this *core* established will help when times get tough. We are all human, and we all can be guilty of improper responses to any given trial. This last chapter will list some simple ideas we can implement to help us get back on the right track.

Allow the Bible to dwell in us.

It is clear in the New Testament that Christians are to allow the Bible to dwell in our hearts. *"Let the word of Christ dwell in you richly*

(Col. 3:16). We need to understand the importance of the concept of *dwell* before we can make any useful strategies. If a strategy we develop does not point us to the Bible, then there is little value.

Strong's Concordance defines the word *dwell* as "to live with" or "to live in."[1] It has the idea of permitting the Word of God to be at home in our hearts.

To understand what this looks like practically, we must know *what* the Bible teaches and then be *ready* to apply it—in a flash—because we have permitted the truth of God's Word to inhabit our heart. Our heart must be hospitable to God's Word, at our *core*, and allow it to readily challenge our thinking and responses to our bumps.

I know it is easier said than done when someone encourages us to apply Scripture. We have all been told to buckle down and do what the Bible says. We have heard it all. *Have faith in God; everything will be okay! Afterall, doing this is what brings peace, right?* We know this to be true, but in the middle of a troubling (or annoying) circumstance, we sometimes stumble.

Technological "Helps"

Some may struggle with focus during Bible reading. If this focus issue is a result of technological temptations (such as scrolling through apps instead of reading your Bible on your phone while you are still in bed), there are, ironically, technological helps. For example, there is the "Pause Pillow". Online, it is described as a "smart pillow that jams wifi signals when in use, to help reduce dependency from social media...when the user lies on the pillow, the pressure sensor inside the pillow causes the Wi-Fi module embedded in Pause Pillow to send a jamming signal."[2] Interesting!

There are also devices that control internet usage in your home. This sounds ideal for parents to use on their teens, but these devices may benefit some adults, too. Amazon has a device and subscription service that can literally *pause* the internet. It is called Circle Home Plus. One of the uses of this product is that you can pause internet service on your multiple devices.[3] I think it is safe to say that this will keep internet interruptions at bay if you use your phone for Bible reading.

For me, a cheaper method is to read from my Bible reading app (while still in bed typically!) and then put my phone down farther away until I am done praying. Otherwise, I will be distracted by looking at the weather and overnight news.

We ought to let the Bible permeate every segment of our life so that the Holy Spirit can help us control our thoughts, words, and deeds. So, any of the following strategies should be geared to help us keep God's Word embedded in our hearts.

Have go-to verses.

Bible-reading plans are great. They allow for planned, organized reading so that the Bible can be read through (in a year, for example). I have found, though, that there are times in life that I need very targeted Bible reading. I think back to when my children were babies and toddlers. These were spiritually stretching times for me. I did not necessarily need to read through three chapters a day in Ezekiel, for example. (Please know that I am not being heretical!) During specific and trying times, I needed to read and reread *very particular* Bible verses. I had to *dwell* on a few verses instead of reading through the whole Bible during those bumpy times.

For example, I had to dwell 1 Corinthians 13, the *Love Chapter*, or I had to concentrate on certain Proverbs for watching my speech with my children. If my young children were driving me *bonkers,* I chose to hum certain Bible verses instead of spewing out an unloving response. Well, I was guilty of the latter for sure, but my goal was to hum the Bible verses instead.

I have found that when I really concentrate on specific passages that deal with my heart's sinful bent toward precise issues, this is when I move toward spiritual victory.

Some specific examples for incorporating our go-to verses in our daily lives is to write the Bible verse(s) on paper and tape to a mirror at home or your vehicle's dashboard. You can also use dry erase markers to write a verse on any mirror. This makes for more efficiency if you want to change out what verse is written.

Reading and knowing about the Bible, as a whole, is vital. We eventually do need to read more than our go-to verses. In a hard trial, though, targeted Bible reading by topic has value.

Incorporate Christian music.

Music can be a powerful strategy to implement during the difficult times in life. Throughout the Psalms, much is listed about praise. We see specifically that it is a good and precious thing to praise God (Ps. 147:1).

We can praise God with instruments and our very breath (Ps. 150:3-6).

I could have filled this whole last chapter with Bible passages that deal with music, singing, or playing of instruments. We see from these previous verses that the Bible says *it is good* to sing praises to God. Putting our focus on God, through the medium of music, keeps us from viewing our trials in such a negative light.

<u>Importance of Colossians 3:16</u>

"Let the word of Christ dwell in you richly in all wisdom, teaching and admonishing one another in psalms and hymns and spiritual songs, singing with grace in your hearts to the Lord" (Col. 3:16).

Regarding Colossians 3:16, my dad pointed out to me that we can teach and encourage others by using spiritual songs. We sing to the Lord, with grace in our hearts, and this can be an encouragement to those around us.[4]

My mom, Debbie Christopher, wrote a blog several years ago called *Light Thoughts*. I recall one of her posts about Colossians 3:16. She wrote, "verse 16 encourages us to sing with gratitude in our hearts. This thankful attitude becomes so much a part of us that it spills out of our hearts in the songs that we sing as we go about our day."[5]

Since godly music is clearly encouraged in Scripture (and is beneficial to keep our focus on God), we certainly can incorporate strategies using music.

An easy-enough use of music is to have Christian music playing in the car on your commute or while doing errands. When I am able, I will play music on my phone from our church's most recently recorded service. Then, without even trying, I have these songs in my mind throughout that day.

I mentioned the following thoughts in a previous chapter. Using Bible verses that have been put into songs is a neat way to keep the Bible in the forefront of our minds. If we start to have a complaining attitude, for example, we can think of Psalm 118:24: "This is the day that the LORD has made..." and sing it in our minds (or out loud). Philippians 4:4 is another verse put to song: "Rejoice in the Lord always..." These are good, solid verses to help recalibrate our discouraged hearts on any given day.

It does not matter if the way you incorporate Christ-honoring music into your own life is completely different than what your neighbor at church does, for example. My church friend, Aimee, chooses to play Christian music over her home's speaker system. I enjoyed hearing the music when I went to her house. Others may not do well in their daily tasks if they had constant music playing at their own homes. The point is that the Bible teaches *it is good* to sing praises to God. We can be totally creative how we do this.

<u>The Mullett Family</u>

There was a stretch of time in the last year that my husband was having to work double shifts and be out late several nights a week. After my children went to bed, I would often watch YouTube videos based off music playlists from our church. On one of those nights, I found a music video by the Mullett Family.[6] The video showed hardships through which the family had gone. Yet, they were able to put out a music video that praised God and His plan.

I later learned how this family travels around the country, performing and singing Christian music at different venues. They are an example of how music, sung from the heart (despite the trials at hand), can keep the focus on God and not on self.

My husband bought me their book for Christmas. In their book, *Big Mountain Bigger God*, Duane and Cindy Mullett wrote about how their firstborn had heart transplant surgery at eight months old and was then diagnosed with congestive heart failure and coronary artery disease as a teenager. He would not survive. Another daughter also needed a heart transplant as a baby. In their book, they wrote:

"Although the health crises they have faced with Austin and Alisha have been hard and emotionally wrenching, Duane and Cindy know that God can be trusted in every circumstance. Despite the unexpected turns their lives have taken, God's "track record" of faithfulness gives them confidence to face the future."[7]

Despite their family trauma, the Mulletts still choose to sing. How amazing!

Surround yourself with good company.

God-honoring friends are a *must*. As children, we were probably taught the principle that bad friends can bring us down (1 Cor. 15:33). Here is another important verse to consider, as it explains the care we must take for *where we receive* our *counsel*.

King Solomon wrote, "...the counsels of the wicked are deceitful" (Prov. 12:5). In our context, we should think about the *counsel* we choose to receive during our trials.

This is not to say that we cannot have friends that are of different spiritual beliefs. Jesus dined with people of different beliefs. It is important, though, that we have like-minded friends that will push us to godly living and encourage us spiritually. This is important, especially if we find that we need additional spiritual help in our *self-counsel.*

Hopefully, a good church home will bring about godly connections. Perhaps you have family that uplifts you. Praise God if there is a godly friend at work or at school.

I am thankful for some good, solid Christian ladies that God has brought along my path. One has encouraged me greatly with just one simple text. With permission, I use her first name. Rhoda and her family were going through trying times. Rhoda had such a beautiful response in the middle of immense hardships. She and I were texting one night, and she made the most profound statement. She typed: "If God allows, it must be good." Years have gone by, and I have never forgotten those words. A godly friend will positively challenge us.

If you mess up or struggle, continue on!

I get weekly joke emails from *Pastor Tim's Cybersalt Digest.* Here is a funny joke from December 2020, titled, *Good Christmas Intentions.*

A kindly 90-year-old grandmother found buying presents for family and friends a bit much last Christmas. So she wrote out checks for all of them to put in their Christmas cards. In each card she carefully wrote, "Buy your own present" and then sent them off. After the Christmas festivities were over, she found the checks under a pile of papers on her desk! Everyone on her gift list had received a beautiful Christmas card from her with "Buy your own present" written inside-- without the check![8]

I laughed when I first read this joke. It shows we are all *human*! Whatever you do on this journey called life, do not give up. Mistakes will happen; you will falter. Do not give up. Seek forgiveness from God and with whomever it is due, and then move forward, utilizing your creative plans to stay on track. Whatever you do, do not give up!

Book's Concluding Thoughts

In life, remember what is *core*.

1. God is sovereign.

2. Trials have purpose.

3. Our faith must stay rooted in God (the result of #1 and #2).

4. Our heart can cause problems.

5. Perseverance is necessary on our journey.

Plus, remember to strategize to stay on track (or to get *back* on track).

A Frustrating Process!

I used to *really* struggle at the grocery store when I had to use those plastic bags for meat or produce. It was terrible and embarrassing. I assumed I was the only one who struggled with these. To make matters worse, my then seven-year-old daughter was shopping with me one day and opened them up with ease. She even told me how *easy* it was.

Thankfully, on another occasion, there was a lady (by the zucchini) who gave me hope I was not the only one who had such struggles! She told me that she could not efficiently figure out how to open those bags.

No matter how long it took us, this stranger and I did not give up on our goal of opening produce bags. I do not know about that lady's motivation, but I had a good reason to stay the course. I absolutely was not going to put my produce on the conveyor belt without them being in the protection of the bag.

I finally got the hang of opening these bags. I figured out that I was being too gentle with them. I just had to find my groove. I sometimes still come across a bag that gives me real trouble, but I press on!

Here is the point: we all struggle at times with our different responses to life's difficulties, even if others do just fine with a similar trial that throws *us* for a loop. Yet, we are not alone in the fact that temptations to respond poorly will strike. We can *drive through our bumps*, graciously, with God's strength. With His strength, and hard work on our end to apply Scripture, we will get our spiritual groove in our specific bumps—even if it means getting critical help along the way! Let us proactively and intentionally keep our spiritual *core* strong.

Application Thoughts for Chapter 11

1. How are you making sure God's Word is at home in your heart?

2. What are some *specific-to-you* strategies to help you respond well in a particular bump?

3. Are there areas where you have spiritually compared yourself to another and then became discouraged as a result? Please give these concerns over to God in prayer. It is important to remember that each person struggles in some area. None of us fully *has it together*!

4. What *core* goal(s) do you have? I encourage you to write out any necessary plans to keep you on course. It is okay to seek out help along your journey!

ACKNOWLEDGEMENTS

KELLY AND SHARON are grateful for the individuals who made this book possible.

Thank you to the professionals at Xulon PRESS who brought us through the publishing process. From Jason Caron, who started the process on the publisher's end, to our pre-publishing representative, Danielle Sarta, and to our editorial help, Greg Dixon and Danielle Babcock Sapienza, thank you for your timely assistance and for bringing us through the process. Thank you to Jesse Kline for the marketing guidance. It was a blessing to work with your Christian publishing company.

I (Sharon) thank God for His countless provisions of grace, even when I respond poorly to my own life's bumps.

I am tremendously thankful for my family's support. Thank you to my husband who worked out many technological kinks for me. From my printer woes to my formatting malfunctions, you were patient through many mishaps!

Mom and dad, I am grateful for your sound help in this writing process. You were often a sounding-board for my thoughts, and you gave me continuously insightful suggestions. Your love for writing has rubbed off on me.

Here is a shout-out to my young children. You keep me on my toes and on my knees (in prayer). You have been sweet to genuinely wonder how things were going with my book.

I am forever grateful to my former graduate school professors. Here is a heartfelt thank you to Greg Christopher (dad!), Kevin Carson, Stephen Schrader, Wayne Slusser, Arnie Smith, and the late Myron Houghton. I am thankful for how God used each of you to play such an important role in my life. You not only taught me theology, but you taught me the importance of applying it at the heart level.

I am also appreciative of those in my life who have contributed to this book in some way. Thank you to Rosalie Francetich, Angie Chance, Heather Rivera, Brad Williams, Brittney Pauley, Dave Perry, Matt Vanderford, Rhoda, and Aimee. Thank you to the Pastors I know and whom I quoted in this book. To Bob Carlson, Phillip Housley, and Dean Clarkson, you are appreciated.

Thank you to Lindsay Clarkson for taking my professional photograph. Thank you to Lori Lasco for getting me professionally ready for the photo shoot.

I want to thank our Book Launch Team:

Nancy Barnes
Jennifer Burrows French
Debbie Christopher
Emily Christopher

Gregory T. Christopher, PhD
James Christopher
Cheri Cilli
Brenda Dugan
Tracy Eckman
Maggie Hatfield
Rhonda Hayes
Cheryl Hipsher
Mandy Horn
Stephanie Housley
Lisa Lawrence
Jannette Malone
Becky Mitchell
Cheryl Page, MS CCC/SLP, ED
Wilma Peninger
Joanne Scigliano
Courtney Shawhan
Tracy Tritt, RN
Maria Warriner

ABOUT THE AUTHORS

SHARON CZERWIEN RECEIVED her Bachelor of Science in Elementary Education (2005) and later her Master of Arts in Church Ministry (2008) from Baptist Bible College and Graduate School. Her area of concentration in her MA program was Biblical Counseling.

She was an adjunct faculty member at Baptist Bible College (2006-2014). She has co-led and taught in several ladies' retreats. She created her blog, Bumps Are Okay, which can be found at www.bumpsareokay.com. She also blogs for Rose Marketing Solutions.

Sharon is married and greatly enjoys homeschooling her two children. She is thankful for her husband being the prized technological and artistic tool in the family's homeschooling toolbox!

Kelly Dean received her Master of Science in Physical Therapy (1997) from the University of North Dakota. She is the Founder of The Tummy Team® and is a Core Rehabilitation Specialist. She teaches online classes that help her clients restore their core.

In her free time, she likes to spend time with her husband and three kids. She also enjoys working with girls in her church's youth group and swimming competitively.

You can follow Kelly at www.thetummyteam.com.

Endnotes

Chapter 1

1. The Tummy Team® can be found at https://online.thetummyteam.com/.

Chapter 3

1. Kelly Dean, chapter 2.

2. Merrill F. Unger, The New Unger's Bible Dictionary, ed. R.K. Harrison (Chicago: Moody Press, 1988), 1214.

3. Stephen R. Schrader, "JOB: The Structure and Purpose, The Dogma of Divine Retribution, Legal Metaphors, and Irony, Part II" (lecture, Baptist Bible Graduate School Chapel, Springfield, MO, October 14, 2005).

4. Schrader, "JOB: Part II".

5. Greg Christopher, "Ecclesiastes" (sermon, Berean Baptist Church, Bolivar, MO, early 2000s).

6. Eugene E. Carpenter, Warren Baker, and Spiros Zodhiates, The Complete Word Study Bible, found on the Olive Tree Bible App, Olive Tree Bible Software (AMG Publishers).

7. Eileen Berry, Heritage Studies 2 (Greensville, SC: BJU Press, 2014), 92.

Chapter 4

1. Angie Chance (Angie Kerans Chance) "Mitch spilled scalding hot tea on my leg first thing this morning! Then, as I'm in the shower...," Facebook, February 10, 2021, https://www.facebook.com/angie.k.chance.

2. Rosalie Francetich, Biblical Counseling Session, Road to Emmaus Biblical Counseling Center, March 24, 2020.

3. Francetich, Counseling Session.

4. Kevin Carson, "Counseling James" (lecture, Baptist Bible Graduate School, Springfield, MO, June 5, 2006).

5. Carson, "Counseling James".

6. Carson, "Counseling James".

7. Brad Williams, interview by author, April 17, 2021.

8. Carol Stock Kranowitz, The Out-of-Sync Child Has Fun, Activities for Kids with Sensory Processing Disorder (New York: Penguin Book, 2003), 132.

9. Kranowitz, The Out-of-Sync Child, 132.

10. Warren W. Wiersbe, The Wiersbe Bible Commentary, NT (Colorado Springs: David C. Cook, 2007), 896.

11. Robert A. Carlson, "Out of the Desert Into New Life" (sermon, Brush Prairie Baptist Church, Vancouver, WA, February 28, 2021).

12. Carlson, "Out of the Desert". Photo credit Lindsay Clarkson.

13. Wiersbe, Commentary, NT, 851.

Chapter 5

1. PAW Patrol, season 7, episode 2a, "Pups Save Election Day," directed by Charles E. Bastien, aired October 30, 2020, on Nick Jr., https://pawpatrol.fandom.com/wiki/Pups_Save_Election_Day.

2. Kevin Carson, "Local Church and Counseling" (lecture, Baptist Bible Graduate School, Springfield, MO, April 6, 2006).

3. Phillip Housley, "Day in the Life of Jesus" (sermon, FB Live, Park Crest Baptist Church, Springfield, MO, March 15, 2020).

4. Housley, "Day in the Life of Jesus".

5. William J. Gaither, "Because He Lives," in The Worshipping Church, A Hymnal (Carol Stream, IL: Hope Publishing Company, 1990), 238.

6. John F. Walvoord and Roy B. Zuck, eds., The Bible Knowledge Commentary, NT (Colorado Springs: Victor Books, 1987), 692.

7. Spiros Zodhiates, ed., The Complete Word Study Dictionary, NT (Chatanooga, TN: AMG Publishers, 1993), 748.

8. Elizabeth George, A Woman's Walk With God, Growing in the Fruit of the Spirit (Eugene, OR: Harvest House Publishers, 2000), 45.

9. George, A Woman's Walk, 50.

10. Eileen Berry, Heritage Studies 2 (Greensville, SC: BJU Press, 2014), 89.

Chapter 6

1. Stephen R. Schrader, "JOB: The Structure and Purpose, The Dogma of Divine Retribution, Legal Metaphors, and Irony" (lecture, Baptist Bible Graduate School Chapel, Springfield, MO, October 2005).

2. John F. Walvoord and Roy B. Zuck, eds., The Bible Knowledge Commentary, OT (Colorado Springs: Victor Books, 2004), 720.

3. Stephen R. Schrader, "JOB: Part II".

4. These were from side notes I wrote from Schrader's "JOB: Part II" sermon. I give him the credit for the thought.

5. Matt Vanderford, lesson series on Ruth, early 2020.

6. Earl D. Radmacher, Ronald B. Allen, and H. Wayne House, eds., Nelson's NKJV Study Bible (Nashville: Thomas Nelson, 1997), 1813, 1995.

7. Elizabeth George, A Woman's Walk With God, Growing in the Fruit of the Spirit (Eugene, OR: Harvest House Publishers, 2000), 69.

8. George, A Woman's Walk, 72.

Chapter 7

1. Joshua Rogers, "Thank God for That Awful Lady in the Lexus," FOX NEWS, December 2, 2016, https://www.foxnews.com/opinion/thank-god-for-that-awful-lady-in-the-lexus accessed 2-18-21
He also blogs at www.joshuarogers.com.

2. Spiros Zodhiates, ed., The Complete Word Study Dictionary, NT (Chatanooga, TN: AMG Publishers, 1993), 819.

3. Kelly Dean, chapter 2.

4. Warren W. Wiersbe, The Wiersbe Bible Commentary, OT (Colorado Springs: David C. Cook, 2007), 1057.

5. James Strong, The Strongest Strong's Exhaustive Concordance of the Bible (Grand Rapids, MI: Zondervan, 2001), 1890.

6. Merrill F. Unger, The New Unger's Bible Dictionary, ed. R.K. Harrison (Chicago: Moody Press, 1988), 544.

7. Tim Keeter, "Hope & Fear For Handling Sinful Anger" (lecture, ACBC Conference Notes, 2017).
This chart can also be accessed on the following website by clicking on the "PDF Notes".
https://biblicalcounseling.com/resource-library/conference-messages/addressing-sinful-anger/. Used by permission via email January 7, 2021.

8. Strong, The Strongest Strong's, 1971.

9. Strong, The Strongest Strong's, 1918.

10. Eugene E. Carpenter, Warren Baker, and Spiros Zodhiates, The Complete Word Study Bible, found on the Olive Tree Bible App, Olive Tree Bible Software (AMG Publishers).

11. Bruce K. Waltke, The Book of Proverbs (Grand Rapids, MI: William B. Eerdmans, 2004), 297.

12. Waltke, Proverbs, 298.

13. Waltke, Proverbs, 91-92.

14. More information can be found at http://www.glensgizmos.com/.

15. Joel Thomas, "Frog Dissection" (lecture and lab, Glen's Gizmos, Vancouver, WA, February 25, 2021).

16. Matt Quinn, "The Pericardium" Teach Me Anatomy, accessed February 26, 2021, https://teachmeanatomy.info/thorax/organs/heart/pericardium/.

17. Quinn, "The Pericardium."

18. Quinn, "The Pericardium."

19. Elizabeth George, A Woman After God's Own Heart (Eugene, OR: Harvest House Publishers, 2006), 59.

Chapter 8

1. Kevin Carson did this water bottle illustration at Baptist Bible Graduate School, Springfield, MO, approximately in 2006.

2. Elyse Fitzpatrick, Idols of the Heart, Learning to Long for God Alone (Phillipsburg, NJ: P&R Publishing, 2001), 25.

3. Fitzpatrick, Idols, 23.

4. Thank you to Randy and Sarah Lang for teaching me about grow lamps while preparing a retreat lesson.

5. Dave Perry taught this illustration at Berean Baptist Church, Bolivar, MO, approximately in 2007.

6. Dean Clarkson, "Psalm 119:11" (sermon, Amazing Grace Baptist Church, Hazel Dell, WA, 2016).

7. D. Martyn Lloyd-Jones, Studies in the Sermon on the Mount (Grand Rapids, MI: William B. Eerdmans, 1976), 92.

8. Lloyd-Jones, Studies, 94.

Chapter 9

1. Stephanie Madrigal and Michelle Garcia Winner, SUPERFLEX...A Superhero Social Thinking Curriculum (Santa Clara, CA: Think Social Publishing, 2008).

2. Prism Pediatric Therapy's website is http://prismpediatrics.com/index.html.

3. Madrigal and Winner, SUPERFLEX.

4. Warren W. Wiersbe, The Wiersbe Bible Commentary, OT (Colorado Springs: David C. Cook, 2007), 908.

5. Wiersbe, Commentary, OT, 930.

6. Wiersbe, Commentary, NT, 838.

7. Associated Press, "Kobe Bryant Helicopter Tried to Climb to Avoid Clouds Before Crash," The Oregonian, January 28, 2020, https://www.oregonlive.com/nation/2020/01/kobe-bryant-helicopter-tried-to-climb-to-avoid-clouds-before-crash.html.

8. Associated Press, "Kobe Bryant Helicopter."

9. Associated Press, "Kobe Bryant Helicopter."

Chapter 10

1. Sandra Bircher, Gina P. Bradstreet, and Christine J. Thomas, English 2 Writing and Grammar, 3rd ed. (Greenville, SC: BJU Press, 2017), 254.

2. Photo credit Lindsay Clarkson.

3. Janet and Geoff Benge, Adoniram Judson, Bound for Burma (Seattle: YWAM Publishing, 2000), 51.

4. Association of Certified Biblical Counselors, "About ACBC," accessed January 21, 2021, https://biblicalcounseling.com/about/.

5. Heather Rivera, "Mental health is hard in general..." Facebook, February 2021, https://m.facebook.com/story.php?story_fbid=2859390474334743&id=100007914551797.

6. Rivera, "Mental health..."

7. Kelly Dean wrote this concept during the writing phase.

Chapter 11

1. James Strong, The Strongest Strong's Exhaustive Concordance of the Bible (Grand Rapids, MI: Zondervan, 2001), 2013.

2. The Pause Pillow can be found at https://globalgradshow.com/?project=pause-pillow, accessed January 25, 2021.

3. The Circle Home Plus can be found at https://www.amazon.com/Circle-Parental-Controls-Internet-Devices/dp/B07QQHRB8P accessed March 21, 2021.

4. Greg Christopher, phone conversation, December 2020.

5. Debbie Christopher, "When Thanksgiving Becomes Our Motivation," Light Thoughts (blog), November, 21, 2011, www.debbiechristopher.blogspot.com.

6. The Mullett family music video can be found at https://www.youtube.com/watch?v=9wcLZa33OyI.

7. Duane and Cindy Mullett, Big Mountain Bigger God, When You are Weak He Will Carry You (Newburg, PA: MileStones International Publishers, 2011), xxi.

8. Tim Davis, "Good Christmas Intentions," Cybersalt Digest (email subscription), December 17, 2020.

CPSIA information can be obtained
at www.ICGtesting.com
Printed in the USA
BVHW081518300921
617854BV00004B/160